A Tree in the Woods

Plato and the Ematomic Dilemma

Waldo E. Forbes

2nd Edition

A Tree in the Woods

2nd Edition
with margin notes

ISBN: 978-0-578-20335-5

Printed in USA

For my dearest wife Jo, our children and their families

Table of Contents

Preface

We humans are perplexing and contradictory. We think all the time, so we ought to realize that others also think all the time. We are bombarded with the thoughts of others which we accept or reject based on trust, a trust we do little to verify.

Stumbling blocks

Each of us knows that we can figure out meaning better than anyone else. We are secure in our clarity. The very idea that we might miss important facts or interpretations is incomprehensible and unacceptable. But our human history is a legacy of misses. Nevertheless, we believe ourselves to be the exception.

This book is an exploration of some scientific reasons for our approach to life in relationship. Following the example of Plato, conversation is the vehicle, with an invitation to the reader to join in. Rules are needed for honest conversation. The rules differ based on the purpose of the dialog. Both parties share responsibility for deciding upon them.

Rules of conversation

Self-assurance closes minds, as does lack of clarity about the rules being used. Our motives are fickle. We mix-and-match the rules and our roles. We use words and phrases which may be too simple or too complex or too rude for the setting. Rules and purposes are human constructs we choose; our survival depends on properly picking them even as we hide our motives. But facts remain facts, whether or not we know or understand or accept them.

The rules of both science and philosophy, which most ignore, require clearly identified premises. Premises must be self-evident, but self-evidence can be a challenging conversation itself, easily confused with self-assurance. My two simple premises can easily seem to make the obvious obvious, which complicates the conversation. Nothing is harder to analyze and discuss clearly than the obvious.

The role of premises: the obvious

Role for objects and observers

First, our world of objects in motion exists (with the four words "world," "objects," "motion" and "exists" defined in the broadest possible sense). Second, more than one observer exists. I am one. Both of us are able to perceive and to think abstractly relative to both the objects and to their motion. For completeness, the observers must have the ability to express their thoughts and to convert them into actions. These premises are *efficient*; they are also *sufficient* for any proof about reality. Whether both are *necessary* would require a dissenter to provide a smaller set which still remains sufficient.

There are immediate consequences. The second premise means that there is neither purpose nor possibility for this paper without the existence of myself and another similar observer.

The first gives the starting point for all physical science. There could not be "objects" unless there exists a "that which keeps objects apart from one another." There must also exist a "that which keeps objects together," else there can be neither "motion" nor a "world." Science calls these "forces." The premises establish both observers and the observed.

How observers play their role

By using the words "that which," both premises suggest that "purpose" is an essential element of proof, which in turn suggests "value" as well; some things are more worthy than others. How? And why? Science generally avoids the why; philosophy explores both. My middle ground is to make the reader aware of the problem, and the need to apply both premises at all times. In saying or implying "must," one accepts the hazards of purpose and value in considering what constitutes "proof."

Both premises also require a notion of "one," but neither makes other demands on either number or dimensionality, both being abstract constructs. They only require an observer who can create constructs. In order that this paper follow any rules of discourse which have been agreed upon, the reader is the one to decide, and to determine either validity or usefulness for any part of the discussion.

The two premises are interrelated through the word "exists." As part of a premise, it only needs definitional clarity, not explanation nor beginning nor end. An object exists if it can be perceived (in the language of science, if it has mass or energy or both). For an object to exist, all observers must be able to separately perceive it, no matter the means they use through their multiple sensory capabilities.

Characteristics of observers: who qualifies

Living organisms are a reality. They might serve as observers. They are called "living" in part because they can perceive other objects using one or more of five senses: sight, hearing, smell, taste and touch. Some or all can communicate. Non-living organisms with similar abilities are not excluded as potential observers. I select humans for their distinguishing feature of "human-ness," with the additional and separate ability to transform their sensory receptions into separate things in and of themselves, thereby making constructs. It is a different ability from the five sensory ones. In the words of J.W.F. Piaget, humans have an ability to "think abstractly," connecting and processing their sensory receptions into new perception(s). One evidence is language; another is use of communication aids such as clothing, maybe brain-waves. Such action by other organisms seems reflexive, not cognitive. A description of "human-ness" as the extra ability to think abstractly gives definitional clarity, as required of any premise, without need of explanation. Nor does it exclude future possibilities. Computers can mimic this ability and might be potential observers. If so, neither definitions nor premises change.

I choose the word "constructs" for the products of abstract thinking. They are distinct from objects because

Definitional clarity: constructs

they are not physically separable from the observer in whom they reside. They are inescapably intertwined with that one observer. Once separated, if written down for example, they then become normal objects, first created as constructs but losing that nature once outside their initiator. Other observers can then observe the object, but have no way of knowing whether or not it has the same reality that it had while only inside its creator. Unlike objects, motion is not an identifiable nor relevant characteristic for constructs. Even if science comes to modify these notions, the second premise merely says that observers have the ability to think abstractly, to perceive, to analyze, to communicate and to create constructs, called "human-ness" in these conversations. A world without an observer is as silent as a remote tree falling in the woods.

Alternate premises: a role for God?

A more compact set which might permit proofs about reality is the *single* premise that God exists. As premise, it requires definitional clarity, being pointless to define a God (or gods) without four characteristics: permanence, knowledge, power and omnipresence. If limited or circumscribed or incomplete in any way, it does not serve usefully. If a marble statue in my garden is my chosen god, then it clearly exists! If the natural world or humankind is my God, it has both permanence and knowledge only through the tautology of saying that it does.

If God exists, then he can easily create both the observers and the observed, my two premises. Many religionists take just such a stance. But for any exploration of our world, nothing about its reality can be verified from this premise. *"It is as it is because God made it that way"* is the same as tautology. Effect, even if agreed upon, is insufficient to prove cause. Proper proof requires both necessity and sufficiency. One can use God as the sole premise if one chooses, but for exploration, the usefulness of such a premise seems doubtful; all questions are answered before even being asked.

An alternative is another *single* premise: that God does not exist. But that premise does not allow deduction of even the simplest parts of reality, namely that objects and motion exist. Or that I and at least one other observer exist—where did either come from? By choosing this alternative, one must then have a set of three premises: both observers and the observed are also necessary. The question changes to whether we can simplify and remove one of the three premises by proving it from the other two. I think not, but leave it to skeptics to explore.

If something cannot be proven from the stated premises, then knowledge of its existence or non-existence can only be by further premise. This paper will show one fact, namely that God *does not exist,* which cannot be proven from my two premises. Equally, it will show that another fact, namely that God *does exist,* cannot be proven either. That such a question cannot be answered is consequential; there are ardent and vocal advocates for each proposition.

Questions that cannot be answered

The *certainty* that the existence of God can be neither proven nor disproven from a reasonable set of premises is useful. For me, and for the body of philosophical inquiry, one way or the other, there *must* be underlying factual truth to the existence of a God or gods. A vacillating state is not possible, given the characteristics such an entity must possess. The certainty frees us to weigh as we choose the meaning of such existence for our lives and actions. There are always consequences for flawed or erroneous choice(s) of premise. Impacts or non-impacts on phenomena of the world are less important than the impact on ourselves of the choice which only we can make. We are individual beings. Impacts will happen (or not) regardless of our beliefs. As implied by

Facts remain facts

the great thinker A.L. Huxley, facts remain facts, whether or not we perceive or know or accept those facts.

Reality underlies everything but may or may not be quite the same as what we think we perceive in the natural world.   There are basic questions which we often ignore.   Galileo and Ptolemy saw different realities because they answered some basic questions differently than later students.   Faulty assumptions have historically led to silly answers.

Abstract thought is a powerful tool

The focus in this paper is on three personages out of respect for thoughts which were likely theirs and which have become a useful way of examining the world.   The value of the three lies outside of the constraints of their era.   Just as art is timeless, we do ourselves injustice when we let such constraints restrict the utility of past ideas.   Plato would not have thought or said the same things several hundred years earlier or later.   But his manner of thinking about any set of 'current' knowledge would likely have carried the same insight, content and kernels which imbue what he actually did record for us. We now have more information and changed method, but neither increase necessarily means that we possess more truth. Things can still elude our gaze.

Change over time is complex

Shifting to my second premise (about constructs), human evolution has two parts, our alive-ness and our human-ness.   Darwinian methods apply to the first, but the second, like the cell multiplication portion of alive-ness, depends solely on the number of constructs available and is exponential.   Darwinian evolution relies on quality more than on number.   Constructs, which are the content and the essence of our human-ness, grow exponentially, each quickly spawning multiple new constructs.   In contrast, change in the *capacity* of human biologic brains is Darwinian, modifying only over millions of years, using the evolutionary mechanism of mutations.   On a human time-scale, the one aspect is essentially static, the other dynamic.   My brain has the same total capacity as Plato's, albeit filled with different things. The same analytical methods cannot be used to understand both content and capacity.

Quality control exists for both, called 'survival.' But quality control for the static and the dynamic necessarily differ greatly. With exponential increase, the number of new items available to become either objects or constructs quickly exceeds any available capacity. For the increase to occur, either perceptions or constructs must be crowded out, which is likely a random process. The changing nature of content may serve as much to distract as to inform, since constructs are readily available to us humans after being objectified. Quality control is the bedrock of successful results; it is wise to separate the Darwinian and exponential processes.

Quality control and survival

These explorations try to transcend difficulties caused by basic questions which underly multiple disciplines, looking at them in a useful way. We tend to get bogged down either in a frame of reference or in a mindset which restricts what we open our minds to consider. The purpose here is to open doors for exploration rather than to bury a reader in layers of abstraction. The attempt itself has value.

Our paradigms

As suggested before, there are questions which cannot be answered under any particular set of premises. *Why* they cannot is legitimate to explore. Also legitimate is to suggest a change of premise, but not a course to be pursued here. Instead, I believe that these conversations and explorations can open up thought-provoking and instructive avenues for future conversations. The early chapters give what I believe reasonable science or philosophy can accept as proof. In the latter part, some of those avenues are laid out in the form of speculations. In a world conditioned by the intellect and by economics, it is for any reader to suspend personal disbelief or not, to try to get on the same wave-length as an author.

Speculations, facts and subjectivity

"ematomic"

The early parts of these conversations identify three realities which have led other explorers astray. None of the three have been clearly explored in any material I know of. *For clarity, I will add the word "**ematomic**" to our lexicon as a term which compactly describes the three realities (factual truths) in a manner which is both comprehensive and useful.* The realities may seem obvious, but are so obvious that they are overlooked. Previously unidentified or named, they are what keep us separated from the totality of reality. Identified, they provide us choices in our manner of studying and understanding reality.

As will be seen, there are other implications from the proofs given in the book. But clarity is a matter for a reader alone to determine. One must first identify where speculations cloud or clarify the process, for both the reader and the author. Speculations, as well as facts, are part of how we live, but are not demonstrable reality.

A world of objects in motion exists. More than one "human" exists, myself as one. Let us see where those two premises lead. Let us come to understand the *ematomic*. Perhaps we can use the implications to bridge some of the many gaps which divide us.

Personal epiphany for this author, or honest exploration? Is there ever real difference between the two in any presentation by an author?

W. E. F.

CHARACTERS *(in order of appearance)*

SARAH - - - - - - - *well-read, inquisitive, young in spirit*
JOHN - - - - - - - *a man of wide and timeless dimension*
PLATO - - - - *ageless thinker and tireless communicator*
SOLOMON - - - - *the embodiment of wisdom and energy*
EUCLID - - - - - - *purveyor of science and mathematics*

These characters should be considered personages inside a strictly hypothetical context, mere vehicles for conversation and exploration.

Their thoughts and words might or might not reflect a connection to those of others with the same name. As the characters themselves understand and make clear, direct quotes would distract substantively from the integrity of the thinking and the nature of the discourse, for both quoter and quotee, thus best avoided unless pithy or inescapably essential.

For the same reason, critiques of other thinkers are best left to the readers themselves as they review those alternate materials in their full expression by the thinker him or herself. Equally, the readers are the proper ones to decide whether the chosen words and procedures satisfy their own need for understanding and clarity.

Utility for the reader plus endurance over time are the only consequential measures. Neither can be anticipated reliably, and most certainly not by this author in a few short pages.

PRELUDE

Can it happen for the simplest and the most obvious to elude the gaze of even the greatest and the most insightful, leaving opportunity for a flashlight to be redirected in order to cut through the murkiness of excess and complex words?

At School in Athens

SARAH: Have I not met you before? John, is it not? You do get around. I always seem to meet you in a new place.

JOHN: Yes, we have met each other several times. And "John" I shall continue to be. The simple is the best route to learning. Surely we are both here for just that reason? Athens has long been a home for the best teachers and the best learning.

SARAH: That is why I am here, even though that reputation was made some time ago. My hope is that it has endured. It is a special pleasure to sit next to you. I have been hoping for a fellow explorer with whom to wander about this city. Relaxed visits can sometimes lead to as much learning as the formal words of experts, and perhaps more wisdom. Location matters: we defend our own turf.

Places for learning

JOHN: I agree. Let us do so when we can escape this stuffiness. This classroom is amazing, but closed in. Let us move outside to open space and make another start.

JOHN: This air on the streets is much fresher. We can better walk and talk. Perhaps even a glass of wine after a bit. What is on your mind?

SARAH: There are some perplexing basic matters which seem to muddle every idea I get, so I want to know more about those. After spending some time with others who are not as clear-headed as you, I think it wise to first propose some rules, with the hope of keeping our words from wandering too far from the basics which puzzle me. The two of us seem able to get on the same wave-length and to understand each other.

How to converse

JOHN: It takes me a bit more time, but we do have all summer for discourse. We both tend to let our thoughts stray down odd pathways, with ideas which seem to leap into the head of one or the other of us unbidden. Tell me what you have in mind?

Creative artists as sources

SARAH: You and I always seek truth in some form. So let us consider several sources which might prove useful. Each marches to his own drummer, but is not aware of doing so. For creative artists, the primary rule for art, poetry, fiction, music, is to tell a good story. The goal of each is pleasure for an audience, with a focus on action. The truth springs from the product itself and may lack substance.

JOHN: I agree. But there are many other sources.

Cataloguers

SARAH: True. History, biography, journalism are cataloguing pursuits which demand lucid use of outside material, with memory essential. Those practitioners must take care to accurately attribute a source for everything used. Their view of truth explicitly depends on materials taken from others.

JOHN: Surely there are other pursuits?

Craftsmen

SARAH: Story is beautiful and catalog necessary, but I am not skilled at either. Craftsmen follow rules of professionalism for their craft; carpenters, attorneys, teachers and those who govern are craftsmen. Their goal is a successful and satisfactory product for their clients, with truth springing solely out of its usefulness. Everyone hopes that what he produces is useful, but I seek a more general truth. I do not have the skill to be a craftsman, but am willing to be judged by others.

JOHN: So far, we see things in much the same way. I am not a storyteller and I'll let others decide whether I contribute anything of use. So perhaps you wish for a product to sell?

SARAH: Not in the least. Salesmen and politicians use rules of their own temporary devising. Their goals can be personal or directed to others. They learn a language of morality, but any useful truth embodied in their utterances can be elusive.

Salesmen

JOHN: Perhaps they are not good role-models for our pursuit of truth?

SARAH: Some see preachers in the same way, but it is not right to let a bad apple or two spoil the whole lot. There are those who fall short in every endeavor. The actual goal of preachers is revealed or pragmatic truth, with rules usually derived from some form of earlier revelation. They hope to provide spiritual sustenance which allows their hearers to make sounder choices and to find a better moral compass.

Preachers

JOHN: Quite so, but please get to the point. You are a scientist and mathematician, while I pride myself on philosophy. I know that neither of us is expert at either, but surely our goal is the pursuit of demonstrated truth?

Thinkers

SARAH: In a simple statement, we both require a solid starting point and a clearly-stated process, including all rules that will be followed. We might use our own premises or build on the earlier proofs of others. Either way, we need to define any terms as clearly and precisely as we can. Our focus is on actual existence in the real world, not story. We cannot assume agreement with our listeners on any point.

JOHN: I would add that when we use earlier proofs, we should identify them as best we can. For premises, let us stick to ones that seem to be clear and self-evident. Our first goal is to demonstrate truth to our own satisfaction. But best to do so in a way which may compel or encourage others to the same decision and belief about that truth.

Credit where due

Objects in motion

SARAH: For out purpose of discovering truths about the world, I would suggest one premise which defines the observers of the world, and another to define that which is observed, the objects of the world. Surely objects and motion are the essence of everything physical which makes up our world.

JOHN: If I see your point correctly, I can agree. And can add that the essence of ourselves as humans with conscious, thinking minds allows us to be the observers. Language is brought into purview, by the necessity of communicating thoughts and converting them into actions. There must be at least two of us, or our conversations would be pointless.

SARAH: Remember that the choice to use premises has three risks: the premises may not be true; they may themselves be the answer we seek; or we might ignore them, a fault I have.

JOHN: I think our two premises are self-evident. They do not themselves tell us anything about objects, motion, our world, humans or about our minds and their constructs. We can move forward together, trying not to ignore either premise. Separate action is silly.

SARAH: None of the other sources of truth have much necessity for premises, even precise rules.

JOHN: But we are philosophers and scientists. It is right to have sought clarity over starting points.

Proof

SARAH: For proof, both of us like necessity and sufficiency, and prefer efficiency as well. An actual scientist can seldom show something to be absolutely necessary.   Philosophers desire both, but put less emphasis on efficiency, seeming to prefer many words even if fewer might suffice. For ourselves, let us try to be succinct.

JOHN: I seem to remember that you are the wordy one.   What would you like to discuss so that we may continue down a path towards better understanding of the truths about ourselves and the world around us?

SARAH: I would still like to clarify the framework a bit. Here is where I would like to go. Each career pursuit or discipline has certain basic questions. If unanswered, the answers of others can be called into question because of basics which have been by-passed or ignored. Each discipline also has its business questions, but I am happy to leave those to the special experts in that field. Underlying basics also seem to have a great deal of commonalty across disciplines. Their study used to be the focus of philosophers, starting years ago with many from this great city.

Starting points

JOHN: We as people are the ones who have created a structure of disciplines as categories to help us into more concentrated focus. You are right that basic questions get overlooked.   When we are forced into a narrow focus, matters that lie outside of that field of vision seldom enter into our explorations.

Pathways

SARAH: The structure, with its categories, is construct. As humans, we like to get down to business, so it is easy to overlook the structure and essence of a discipline. The structure itself does not yield practical results. But I am interested in the overlooked questions which can lead us astray, not in the ones which arise within the categories.

JOHN: The generality of philosophy is to look at basics, but I am interested in your idea that there might be unexplored and ignored matters outside any restricted vision. Perhaps there are others who can help us.

SARAH: As basics, they may be crucial, ignored or not. Seeking help is prudent. That is why I am here in this very city. First, I want to give you more detail about the kinds of problems I see.

JOHN: If you must. It is early, and everyone considers me endlessly young. I will try to keep my eyes from rolling, or closing.

Natural sciences

SARAH: The business of the natural sciences is to consider and resolve an ever-growing stream of questions which relate to the past, present and future of our own natural world in the context of time and space, and even of all possible natural worlds. Every day we gain more "answers" in the form of theories, understandings and practical applications. We like to debunk the answers of predecessors, but must recognize that too soon the same fate will probably await our own theories. Answers shaped by Euclidean geometry falter if the geometry falters. The existence and nature of a unified field theory,

Cosmology

or an elemental understanding of time and space, still falter today. One can pose and answer a question about the start of the universe without understanding what either "start" or "universe" actually means. The daily work of science may seem independent of such basic answers, but the answers then stand on shaky ground. We tend to feel that our own scaffolding of presumptions is solid and safe. The structure of 'scientific method' gives my fellows comfort today. It is easier to ridicule an earlier structure, the scaffold used by other builders, than to examine our own. If we set aside our egos, which dwell in the now, the durability of any 'city built by man' does not hold promise for lasting durability. A few centuries has been a good run in the past, but pretty short for definitive truth.

JOHN: A bit of a wordy lecture I must say, but even one who does not fully understand your terms can see your point.

Role of mathematics

SARAH: In mathematics, seemingly intractable problems are solved every day. Practical capabilities astound us. But there remains an unanswered nexus between mathematics and the natural world. In what sense are the two intertwined, or are they inescapably separate? That they are mutually beneficial cannot be denied. Does the precise nexus matter? Basic stuff.

JOHN: Again, I agree, but move away from science. We hear daily of its exploits.

SARAH: Religion might seem to focus on the existence and nature of God, and the spiritual side of humankind. *Role of religion* But the daily work of religionists deals with real problems which confront actual individuals and communities, the daily lives of people. It is just viewpoint that a physicist or engineer is more practical than a priest or a lecturer in religion. The answers of the priest stand on the quicksand of unanswered basics. If God, however named, existing or not, differs from the beliefs of the priest, then the practical answers of the priest can lead to harmful error. Religious views and practices have evolved over time, perhaps even more than those of the scientist. Scorn for earlier answers is just as unproductive. I select the term religionists in order to distinguish from theologians. Most of the former tend to have their thinking colored by doctrinal matters. Unanswered basics can be obstacles to ultimate truth, whether the truth is revealed or demonstrated. Doctrine can easily lead to unexamined basics.

JOHN: Yes. It is hard not to accept as well that moral decisions are at the heart of many things. But it is generally conceded that moral issues are not a fertile province for science.

SARAH: Your observation takes us to the human side of scientific exploration. Social scientists deal with *Sociology and* collectives of humans, namely groups. It is challenging *the polis* even to define a group, or *polis*. Due to the individuality of each person, the intractability of business questions about groups has become even more frustrating. Multiple unanswered basics such as the nexus between the human and the non-human, as well as the actual nexus between two separate humans, lurk in the background.   How did any *polis* arise?   Science has not yet figured out how to answer the basic questions and must restrict itself to the practical details, the useful business desire to create systems which can help humans.

JOHN: I am sure that the distinction between "business" and "basic" is not clear-cut for any discipline, let alone how each of us might see it. I do not yet see the details of your concerns, but the outlines are starting to emerge. There are matters which keep our field of vision within disciplines.

SARAH: The risk of avoiding the basic questions is two-fold: to presume that we already know or understand the answers, and to ignore some implications that may be hidden from a narrow view.

JOHN: So far, these are all constructs, but I can see that what you consider 'basic' may actually underlie many disciplines.

Philosophy: how things hang together

SARAH: Philosophy has used many approaches to describe truth, or "what truly is," with the approaches themselves generating ever more questions. In my view, a basic question raised by philosophy relates to subject-object separation and to the impact of viewpoint. Both words and understandings necessarily arise from those approaches. Do I know what I think I know, and what does that mean? Even if I could express a question or an answer perfectly, would it mean or be the same to another person who stands in a different place?

JOHN: The approach of philosophy is no different from that of any other discipline: to try to subdivide and categorize in a way that brings clarity to some question.

SARAH: But that process itself adds layers which may misdirect rather than clarify. As purely human construct, philosophy is especially subject to the implications of human-ness. Philosophers may not see the ships they steer as smooth-sailing vessels, but the shoals of unanswered basics may still founder even the most wary if they focus only on business.

JOHN: I think I see the reason for this walk and for your visit here.

SARAH: As a starting point and to keep our focus on the rules, which is where we started, there are certain words for which we or any student ought to have clear intent. Easy examples are: "infinite", "all" or "every", "no" or "none", or "nothing," plus most aspects of time and space. Even those who would teach are seldom consistent, even internally, in how they use words. True coherence is unlikely without consistency.

Basic words

JOHN: With you as mathematician and myself as philosopher, our senses are probably on high alert.

SARAH: Even as we say that, words which embrace legitimate abstract or complex concepts, such as "proof" which I used earlier, are best left to experts to explore. For our purposes, we can let our audience choose the meaning. But those who answer business questions should explore such things for those they wish to inform.

JOHN: Nevertheless, clarity and consistency in the choices for our own words is still essential. If you say that "all x are y," it is crucial for me to know what your "all" means. Does your word "are" refer to attributes or to essence or to some restricted version of either essence or attributes? So we must do the best we can. And we have the luxury of asking each other as well.

SARAH: Time and matters of size are special traps for cosmology and theoretical physics; equally so for philosophy and religion but more often faced. In contrast, poets and cataloguers have the luxury of avoiding the traps of actual reality as they create beautiful

Time and size

and informative works; careful thinkers ought not. That is our hope and pretense, even without detail. It is tempting and common to say "infinite" when logically one can only mean "very large," a different matter indeed! Is the infinite of our mathematics the same as an existential infinite?

JOHN: A concept I have used many times.

Belief vs truth

SARAH: Over time, ideas can evolve, modify, expand and be refined; an idea becomes useful if its kernel is solid, even if the idea is eventually discarded. Poets become known for a body of their work. For the thinker, the idea is the thing; for the poet or novelist, how the idea is expressed is the essence, not clarity about the idea itself. An observer such as myself merely provides working material for both. You and I participate solely to reach better understanding for ourselves, and perhaps others. We are trying to find truth about our real world. There is a difference between belief and truth. We must be careful not to be deluded by any version of the former into supposing it to be the latter.

JOHN: Well summarized. As fallible humans, we confound the two all the time. Let us have a glass of wine before we catch our breath for another day.

SARAH: Then I shall head for my own more comfortable room, but look for you again tomorrow on these streets. I like the fresh air. It helped me see more clearly. A good start.

A Question for Plato

The Conversations Begin

SARAH: Friend John, what a pleasant surprise to meet you so early, and just as I was reflecting on some recent reading. May I continue with the familiarity you seemed to embrace yesterday?

JOHN: Please do. "John" I shall be. The simple is still the best route to wisdom.

SARAH: It is quite a journey that I have undertaken, mostly of the mind, but with the occasional enticing pleasure of memorable encounters. We spent some time yesterday avoiding the point of my visit here. It had been a while since I saw you, so I thought some basics might be helpful before plunging in. I hope I did not offend?

Difficulties with relationship

JOHN: Dear girl, not so. But my casual greeting may offend as well. Offense can be easily found.

SARAH: Point taken, and forgotten. I am Sarah. Moving on, I know you to be a keen observer, with an ability to recall even things from the distant past. It is just such a talent that I am earnestly in need of today and throughout my visit.

JOHN: How so? Little escapes your penetrating gaze; best that I stay out of range.

SARAH: Not at all. The question which came to mind is one where you once told me of an interesting discussion between two ancients that you had overheard. I would put it to the great Plato himself, if I had the power.

JOHN: Sometimes we are capable of more than we realize.

SARAH: Perhaps, but better the known than the speculative. It is a simple question indeed: do all things have a Form, a word for which Plato had great fondness

Do all things have a Form?

and many writings. I recall that you told me of a discussion of that very matter that he had had with the great Solomon himself. Can you recount for me the details? My memory too often falls short.

JOHN: Your memory astounds, but I think I can relate the matter once again. The exact words may elude me at times, so consider my efforts a sincere re-statement of the thoughts, if not the words. Undue attention to precise wording can be irresponsible distraction rather than useful honesty. But we still must try to use words consistently.

SARAH: You never distract, and are not one to be distracted.

JOHN: It happened that the two of them had just met on the streets of Athens, quite near to where we now stand. Plato was very much the younger of the two, although he never seemed youthful to me. Neither appeared to know the other, nor was either aware of my presence, since I was out of view. Here is the conversation as best I can recall it:

PLATO: Ah dear friend, it is a pleasure to see one on our streets who seems to be an intent student and observer. You appear to marvel at the glories of our beautiful Athens, just as I do.

SOLOMON: How can one not be amazed at its beauty?

PLATO: What fortunate circumstance brings you here? Your raiment suggests that you make your home in some other place?

SOLOMON: I am very much a stranger here, but it gladdens me to be called a friend. My name is Solomon, and I come from the distant city of Jerusalem. Among the many pursuits that have occupied my time, I have been blessed to devote the deepest sort to seeking greater understanding in all matters. I have learned that thorough observation is the only proper starting point. I had heard of a philosopher in Athens named Plato.

PLATO: What a happy chance. Such is my very own name. Understanding has also been my goal, as student and observer. I have long called Athens my home, and have heard many speak of your wisdom. But I thought poetry was your practice?

SOLOMON: Indeed, poetry is truly one of life's pure and honest pleasures. And well suited to my native tongue.

PLATO: In our city, poets take such pleasure in the beauty of their words that they can seem satisfied to weave mere descriptive fabric. That is a departure from true knowledge, at least to the thinking of this poor student. But I have been told that it can be otherwise, with the words coming deep from the heart of some poets. It is pleasing to learn that pursuit of knowledge is how you see your quest. Perhaps your poems just serve to hide a quest which has been in vain?

Poetry

SOLOMON: There is truth to that vanity! But remember that poems are also suited for honest history, a tool which I had heard to be just as common here. Call them poems or history or even myth, I do know that they seem too indirect and incomplete for true knowledge. The fullness of any event, no matter how closely measured, cannot be observed by any one man or single pair of eyes. If observed at all, it must be incompletely so.

Limitations of history

PLATO: That is honest commentary.

SOLOMON: In like manner, I have found that my native tongue serves poorly for expressing truths, even after seeing through the poetry. Our language is better for songs than for the precision of thought and word for which you are known. So my desired pursuit at times seems hopeless. I come to Athens to gain advantage from her teachers. They seem gifted with clarity of thought and expression, doubtless gaining as much from the quality and exercise of their minds as from the capabilities of their native language.

PLATO: You flatter indeed. It may be true that the simple matter of the place and time of our birth does shape our views and abilities. But I suspect less so than appears.

Forms vs names

SOLOMON: Before I agree or disagree, let me state to you my question, using a word that I have heard you call your own. It is a simple thing: do all things have a Form, or merely some of them? Can two share the same Form? In my writings, I have stated my belief that all things which exist have already been named, that they have a name. That idea may differ from your Form for things?

PLATO: By Form, I think you suggest my meaning to be the itself-by-itself of a thing, a singular thing. As such, it is true enough that I do often speak of Forms. I direct thought towards the itself-by-itself in order to make clear the subject of a discussion. You see one thing, but it may seem different to me. Yet we wish to talk about the same object.

SOLOMON: Clarity is all. By putting a name to a thing, we make it separate, and can either hide or expose its true being, which was my intent. I like your phrase, the itself-by-itself. I think that is what I try to name.

PLATO: I had not thought before about the answer to your question, but it merits discussion. Do all things have a Form? Even better because of what you have written. It seems to me that, if everything which exists has a name as you say, then it must also have a Form, the thing itself being the Form with the name merely our way of trying to pin it down for joint conversation and thought.

SOLOMON: Much as I would state the matter. Another way of thinking about the question would be this: between us, we have now used many words. Some we have used several times. If we were truly speaking clearly, each word would mean the same thing each time we used it, also representing the same Form each time. Each group of words would have similar constancy as well, and must derive from the singularity of the object itself. We could list them all at the end of our study. I do not have such skill nor concentration, nor is it possible, but it would be a goal.

PLATO: To return to your question, clearly you must mean all things which have a physical presence in this world, regardless of how we group them in categories or by attributes, things we can touch. My Forms also exist for things whose substance is harder to sense. We cannot easily agree about an object unless we can point to it. Let us set those unclear things aside for now.

Forms vs objects

SOLOMON: That is exactly what I mean. We use all sorts of device to gain clearer insight into the matters of our thought and conversation, but in the end, our target is often the reality and nature of some thing of the world. I can say that I am thinking in my mind of something which is round, but unless I can point to a round object that we both can see, I am simply speaking in riddles; you could not possibly know of what I speak.

PLATO: Quite so. I speak frequently of the Form of things, since that is my quest. But I must use words to do so. I try to clarify my words and thoughts by speaking of the Forms, or of the events and actions being discussed. Events and actions direct the mind to the motion of the object, but are also things of the observable world. I also use attributes and categories, giving examples at every turn, trying not to be distracted by the words which may be many for a single itself-by-itself.

SOLOMON: I too am known for an excess of examples.

Forms vs constructs

PLATO: My analogies are for finding and using the Forms, however indirect the manner of approach. I wrote my entire Apology about the death of Socrates as an explanation of the Form of Wisdom and the life or calling of a philosopher, clearly not a thing to reach out and touch, an object. In Crito, I tried to discover the true Form of my beautiful city, Athens. Alas, I have never been able to discover the true substance of any Form! If faced now with the choice to accept an elusive physical reality, using my poor description as the best I can do, versus supposing the reality itself to be an untouchable ideal, my heart and mind both tell me that the substantial, not the ideal, is a better choice. Otherwise, I would have lots of different types of Forms. The word would create a

A muddle

muddle rather than draw the two of us closer. An uncomfortable change for me, but your question suggests a need to avoid confusion about the simple Form of a tree, clearly reachable and touchable. If I persist in saying otherwise, I perpetuate the muddle. Ideas must be distinct from such objects.

SOLOMON: I too, in using and attaching a name, see potential for distraction and subterfuge if the same name is attached to many differing things.

Difficulties with constructs

PLATO: It is also true that recently I have been trying to narrow down the idea of a Form, with more inclusiveness and hierarchy, each shared by many things. More words and categories again, but trying to blaze a philosopher's pathway towards unity, away from complexity, toward peace for my Soul. It has led me to a simpler view, that an ultimate and unifying Form, a higher one, being that of Beauty, may be the needed measure of true knowledge.

SOLOMON: I would like to think that my mind too is capable of new directions, but that quest seems personal and elusive.

PLATO: Taken thus, the word Form would not have the universality I once insisted on. But your question gives me pause in such a choice. A hierarchy might serve the sake of philosophy but, in doing so, mask the reality of the world. Have you not found that, in using words, our minds can cloud our perceptions as easily as clear away the haze?

SOLOMON: Indeed I have. Why else would there be poetry and story?

PLATO: Perhaps a hierarchy need only exist at some higher level, not being fundamental. It might be clearer to accept that each thing has its own one itself-by-itself. We merely try to tie those together with our words, thus making easier the matter of study and understanding. Both Form and name are constructs of our choosing when applied to objects. The greater number of both Forms and names would still each have a connection to a particular and single itself-by-itself, however elusive to establish.

Hierarchy and clarity

SOLOMON: I can see the risk of taking the simple and unnecessarily building the complex, not allowing each thing to have its proper time and place and moment. And I too, while able to state that everything has a name, have been unable to discover exactly what that means, to put my finger on the separateness of the names from the things. It has seemed to put the essence no closer to discovery.

PLATO: We share the same frustration.

The tree-ness of a tree

SOLOMON: One tree is completely different from another tree, so what is *the tree-ness of a tree*? And how much of that tree-ness is simply my observation and description of it?

PLATO: It did not occur to me to state such a thing although one of my students brought it up. I would now state that matter in a different way: the tree-ness of *each* tree, perhaps for each observer as well, not the tree-ness of *a* tree. A Form for each, but perhaps, in some sense, a higher notion of Form, a grouping. It is hard to use any word in a simple way.

SOLOMON: Once again, I would stay away from too much hierarchy and order. Those risk being our creation, not the essence. The essence is in *each separated thing*, with a name attached.

Untouchable things

PLATO: Your point is well taken. But even so, certain things always seem too distant to search for a Form. What is their reality? I think of the Soul as a matter which must be let go of, leaving it as a creation of the gods which can only be described in story, mostly outside the reach of what can be called a thing. Socrates found himself in such a state with Simmias and Cebes, telling a beautiful story about the Soul but finally giving up on the pursuit of its Form. Having a name, that name may represent a Form, but only constructed in my mind. You and I cannot see that same construct. It is a different matter when we talk about a particular tree.

SOLOMON: Quite so. It is hard to see the physicality of a Soul. But not easy to let go of habits!

Roles of names and Forms

PLATO: It seems clearer to say in that instance, that the name represents an idea in the mind, not a thing of the world that we can put our finger on. Perhaps Soul fits there. Names for ideas in the mind, my constructs, does not seem to establish the clarity that a name for an itself-by-itself does. My idea might have one Form or name, but your idea, using the same word, another. We could never make them meet, not that the frustration would distract us from the pleasure of trying.

SOLOMON: But let us return to the heart of today's matter. Is there any thing for which there is no Form if restricted to the itself-by-itself of an object?

PLATO: Now that you put the matter in that different light, indeed there is not. Unless it has an itself-by-itself that we can both perceive, it is not a thing of the world, only a construct of mine or yours, purely in our mind. As soon as a true thing comes to mind, the fact of its Form is clear, whether or not we use the same name. I spent much time trying to pin down the elusive nature of ideas, even using the word Form. But I can see that there is no real itself-by-itself for such things.

SOLOMON: It seems clear to me that ideas or constructs do not overlap with objects, so there is no need of names for them. It was worth my journey to gain such clarity, to help the puzzle take its shape. To answer your earlier worry, I am now clear that the itself-by-itself of a thing in no way depends on where we find ourselves, be it Athens or Jerusalem.

Non-overlapping sets

PLATO: Nor does it depend on the phrases or words we use to describe it.

SOLOMON: I agree.

PLATO: We can say that each thing has a name, or we can say that each thing has a Form, or we can say that each thing has an essence, but no matter the phrasing, it is a matter of the thing, its being, not of our perception of that thing. Not that the latter may not prove to be of any less value in how we see the essence. Attributes and categories, even if not objects, may have a usefulness.

SOLOMON: Better to consider those as constructs in the mind. We may see an object through a very dark glass, but it is there and it is real and it is one.

PLATO: It may not seem the same to both of us, but each object of the world exists on its own, no matter how we see it.

SOLOMON: It exists alone and does not depend on you or me. I now have solid ground for study and my conversations.

PLATO: So I see the matter as well. It is happy indeed that you should come just now. Perhaps you can stay a while? I have heard rumblings that the immortal gods will finally speak to us more truths. Such insight might help today's uneasy piece of this puzzle find a proper home.

SOLOMON: Alas, you tempt me, but I cannot stay. Many duties call me home. It seems that my tendency to err is intertwined with the skills which have been credited to me; I would rather not add inattentiveness to the list. There will be others who will come to you. This conversation is too important to wither and die. Clearness of expression must become the norm in pursuit of truth. Such is the nub, even if we use too many words.

PLATO: One must ignore both the medium and the messenger, shifting entire focus onto the elusive but omnipresent Forms as I now use that word. Your norm and mine seem to be the same.

Wisdom vs knowledge

SOLOMON: I am going to call my pursuit that of seeking wisdom. Such a word would add discernment and proper application to mere knowledge. Without discernment, I am only a pair of eyes. What a help you have been, friend Plato.

PLATO: I too shall focus on the true substantial essence behind my ideas and words and phrases, undistracted by our normal carelessness of thought and word. Even if I cannot precisely connect a name with the Form or with the thing itself, and must accept a gap between them, so be it.

SOLOMON: My examples show the gaps but barely make a start.

PLATO: Nor do I lack for the new and unexplored. There are so many matters for the good of our Souls and to improve our manner of living, in how we follow our education and manage our cities. My thoughts will turn to those. We cannot waste time befogged in a struggle with a reality we cannot change, unable to reach the actual Form, the itself-by-itself, rather than the word or words we use for it.

SOLOMON: Well said and well decided. We should place a burden on the hearer to discern and to decide intent and meaning, without distraction by our occasional imprecision of description.

PLATO: On another matter, I also want to write about Love which might even bypass the distraction of words. I once heard of a beautiful song that you wrote. I think there is much more to the matter of Love. Perhaps there is even an itself-by-itself for Love, even if it has a different reality that we cannot reach out and touch, but may very well be shared by all of us. I sense that it may even go to our goal of finding Beauty, and shared Truth. Perhaps Love provides a way to bridge these gaps, an elusive glue that can bind us together, a trust?

Love

SOLOMON: As to depth and binding power for Love, I cannot say. My poem was purely from my heart. One value of poetry is to leap beyond the limits of a language. A discussion of Love would take us late into the night and make my journey hard. Another time perhaps?

PLATO: I suppose it must be so. For now, I shall leave the word Form as we have restricted it. Every thing of the world has a Form and a name. Travel well, friend Solomon of Jerusalem!

JOHN: And so they parted. I do not believe they ever saw each other again. My luck was great to overhear. Even as we speak, I once again feel the power of some things they said.

SARAH: Fair enough to see the power, but they certainly did create a muddle!

JOHN: A muddle with no tools available to fix!

SARAH: That is indeed the conversation of which you told me, and my readings may help us. Plato and Solomon gave me clarity on one matter, a direction in which I believe both might have moved over time. I like the idea of a primal Form, being the thing itself, connected to a name as Solomon saw it. A hierarchy is best omitted because there is a one-to-one relationship between names and the primal Forms or things of the world, just as they identified. Each object, or itself-by-itself, has a name, or Form as Plato came to use the word.

Hierarchy

JOHN: The notion of hierarchy confuses, but it had been important to Plato.

SARAH: And they identified the clear separation—a gap—between names or Forms and the things themselves. Maybe a wall. Objects and their names are not interchangeable. The name is easy. But the actual itself-by-itself, while undeniably existing, is unreachable and not nearly as easy. We must be content with a name or best description, plus the knowledge that such is the best we can do.

JOHN: I understand your point, that there is and must be an unbridgeable gap between the itself-by-itself, an object, and what we can experience and describe using names and constructs, the only tools available to us. Plato clearly struggled to find a way to cross the gap, gradually changing and restricting the way he used the word Form as he tried to make the way accessible. To no avail. A dilemma.

Plato's dilemma

SARAH: He started out with a conflict in his use of the word Form. He included both simple objects of the world as well as constructs of the mind. Hierarchy may be useful for the latter, but it is not as promising for focus on the simple itself-by-itself of actual objects where it is hard to see true hierarchy.

JOHN: He started and ended with the elusiveness of the objects themselves. They are independent of their assigned names, but do have properties we seek to understand, the stuff of science

Elusive objects

SARAH: His struggle is a real one; elusiveness is inescapable, and exists on two levels. My recent reading was helpful. There is now well-established truth that no thing can be physically observed with precision, regardless of our words. Thanks to W.K. Heisenberg and others, the position and the velocity of any object cannot be measured or described at the same time. So we must confront both the elusiveness of the object (or Form) itself and the attachment of a name to it.

JOHN: An added dimension to Plato's problem, and no less real. His student Aristotle bypassed the dilemma by ignoring it. The object is there, and that good enough for him! But the dilemma created by words exists, even if ignored.

SARAH: To go back, there is a first unbridgeable gap between the description, no matter how precisely we think to have pinned it down, and the Form, the itself-by-

Gaps

itself. There is a second gap simply because we cannot catch up with the object itself. There is also a third, created by the simple fact that for objects to exist, they must have separation, one from every other. Whether the gaps are viewed in their entirety or separately, they do exist and all are unchangeable reality. It is hard to discuss something which isn't there. My interest lies in the existential gap between the name and the Form, rather than in the two we think we can study. Science daily studies the portion caused by the inability to locate, the Heisenberg portion, and the portion caused by separation, with even entire books about such 'empty' space. For our objectives, it may be best to consider the entirety, all of which is barrier to any type of complete understanding.

Layers of names

JOHN: There is another difficulty which has been mentioned to me by others. If each thing has a name, then that name itself, when written down, is another thing which in turn must have a name. And so on. Where does it end? Perhaps the same problem does not exist for a particular Form, but your one-to-one relationship casts doubt.

SARAH: Indeed, you go to the heart of a matter not clearly formulated by Plato and others. Constructs are not objects of the world but creations; the itself-by-itself for constructs is completely elusive.

JOHN: Please clarify.

"All" and the infinite

SARAH: Today, we speak of the infinite in a most casual manner, and when we use the word "all," we are seldom precise or clear as to whether we mean a finite and countable all or some kind of infinite all. As we have gathered knowledge over the years about how things work in this world, we sometimes confuse the fact of extra knowledge with our ability or inability to understand the actual gaps and separations exposed by Plato and Solomon. I think we too have failed to clearly differentiate constructs of the mind from objects of the world.

JOHN: Surely that would be the only failure we have had? I know philosophers have tried, but do not know the details.

SARAH: By way of example, we can talk casually about a "point," perhaps visualizing a dot on a piece of paper. We would normally mean much the same as Plato might have meant. As a word and thing, it would have a Form. But if we instead think about what a mathematician would mean by using the word "point," we can start to see the difficulty.

A "point"

JOHN: You must explain yourself a bit more clearly.

SARAH: I read a most useful essay by D.L. Sayers, called *The Lost Tools of Learning*, in which she described a point as having ". . . location in space, but without extension." That understanding has existed in many places for a very long time, usually without quite such clarity of expression. Such a point cannot actually exist in the physical world as a discrete entity because of its infinitely small size and its lack of dimensionality. About things, we easily speak of them as being "infinitesimal" in size, meaning that they are very, very small, a different matter entirely from lacking dimensionality. We also now have common words such as "pixel" for certain very small physical points.

JOHN: You are leading towards either confusion or greater clarity of thought. It would be good that we seek some common ground of understanding.

SARAH: Common ground on certain matters of terminology and thinking is crucial.

JOHN: A sentiment I would echo.

The use of models

SARAH: We can use one-dimensional figures such as lines, or planar ones such as circles or triangles to clarify both the infinitely large and the infinitely small. The Form for such constructs, or models if you prefer, can even be independent of size. As constructs, they do not and cannot exist as things. The physical existence for such constructs, which can have aspects we consider infinite, is impossible in the sense of something 'one can reach out and touch.' Yet we mostly tend to ignore the unclear nature or the physical reality of such constructs when we speak about them. The infinite leads us to strange places and is a word thrown out far too casually. But I am turning the discussion in another direction, and far too late in the day for that.

JOHN: Yes, you are indeed taking matters in another direction, and doubtless into yet another set of difficulties. We have come upon quite enough to ponder for today. Let us stick to the gaps between names or descriptions and the itself-by-itself for now, the gaps identified by Plato. We can keep in mind the other gaps which are caused by motion and separation among objects. As barriers to true understanding, the latter force us to turn to constructs and models. Models of that type are no help for the gaps of Plato.

SARAH: You do like to bring me back to ground. We shall sleep well enough with some accomplishments behind us. Good day, then. Let us meet again tomorrow.

Euclid's Puzzlement

A Continuation of the Conversations

SARAH: You are punctual as always. Overnight, perhaps dreams have brought you another conversation from the past to clarify the matters of the infinite?

JOHN: How could you divine such a result? There was indeed another, some time after the one we discussed yesterday, but in a similar situation. Do not think badly of me. I know I have a reputation for lurking in shadows, but my eyes and ears have served me well. I was fortunate to overhear a conversation between Plato and a different ancient, one with great skill in mathematics.

SARAH: Please recount it for me. I spent the night in further reading related to these matters. Together we may come to better understanding, just as we did yesterday.

JOHN: Here is what I recall. Plato had just met Euclid on these streets, with the latter a bit the younger man:

PLATO: My good friend, Euclid of Alexandria, why do I find you here in Athens and so downcast? Surely you have not taken up the elusive study of Forms?

EUCLID: Ah, no, I think not, at least not a Form as you would use the word. Rather I have been thinking of an ellipse, a different kind of form. And seeking advice.

PLATO: Do you mean the generality of an ellipse or a particular instance?

EUCLID: I am not sure, although I see it colored blue, to separate it from what is outside its bounds. Here, I have made a drawing for you. Perhaps I may gain some knowledge and assistance from you?

*True opinion
and the nature
of proof*

PLATO: I do not hesitate to tell you first, dear Euclid, that my mind has been somewhat confused upon learning of a long discussion between my dear teacher Socrates and young Meno of Thessaly. I doubt you have met either since the life of the one has turned far indeed from philosophy, while the Soul of the other is now only in communion with the gods. Their discussion has led me to wonder whether the good of my own Soul would be enhanced if I left off the pursuit of knowledge and merely sought to gain true or right opinion, leaving it for others to attempt to tether my uncertain insights and offerings. Let them call it knowledge or even wisdom, not I.

EUCLID: Somehow, I knew of that confusion. I resolved myself to do much the same. I am proud to believe that many feel I have achieved success in anchoring opinions so as to show their truth, letting them escape the fate of Daedalus' work.

PLATO: Letting anything get away, to escape review by our students, would seem tragic.

Ellipses

EUCLID: I have uneasy peace about this ellipse. I see a certain blue one lying in front of my eyes. I cannot help but ponder that ellipse and what lies inside. As you probably know, I have elsewhere described the smallest thing as a point. My search is to find the fullness of this ellipse in the matter of points. It seems entirely covered by them, and that is the way I would describe it. Most certainly it is covered by a very large number of points. But can the number be counted or is it beyond counting?

PLATO: My past practice would be to seek permission to ask you questions so that we might both gain understanding. However, I have been spoken to by the gods in a manner which suggests that the two of us in honest discussion might reach truth or right opinion. All men know that what comes to us directly from the gods cannot be other than the truth.

EUCLID: That is what I have been taught. Tell me what they told you.

PLATO: I have come to understand that my quest to know the Form of any thing will always fail. The truth of any thing lies in the realm of its finite physical existence, being the itself-by-itself of the thing or object. But it is unreachable with any description. One may physically put one's finger on it, but still not have its name actually be what one is touching. The name is not the actual thing itself. There is a gap. I must be content with right opinion about Forms and names.

Objects vs names and constructs

EUCLID: Now your words do truly confuse me.

PLATO: I shall confuse you more. For now, let us agree that the finite can always be counted. The number may be so large that only the gods can truly comprehend it, but it does exist as a real number. The infinite is the realm of things which cannot be counted or measured. It consists of the infinitely many, the infinitely large and the infinitely small; perhaps an infinite number of different types of infinity, all encompassed within the first. There was a conversation with Protarchus where Socrates suggested just such a thing.

The finite

EUCLID: So, my idea of a point would be an example of the infinitely small, but it is a very useful part of the geometry I have constructed. And my line contains an infinite number of points, proceeding an infinite distance and equally essential to my studies. But now that you point it out, each must be a restricted version of the infinite. The actual infinite would have to encompass both, since nothing could lie outside of a true infinite. Our names, such as "line of infinite length," do not use that word in an accurate way. Our constructs might be very different from true reality, whether a general construct or drawn for you as a picture of what is in my mind.

Constructs have a different reality

PLATO: Quite so. Both are versions of a restricted idea of 'infinite,' and very useful as constructs or models. The precision of detail is for craftsmen, but constructs in the mind are not things of the world which is where my interest today lies.

EUCLID: I seek usefulness. I am no philosopher. Constructs are clearly useful and allow the building of strong temples.

PLATO: We may not be as far apart as you suggest.

EUCLID: Such is the conviction of any good teacher.

All objects are countable

PLATO: Both viewpoints may serve us well, for usefulness and clarity. The next message from the gods was this: in the world in which we live, all things are name-able, so countable, and finite The infinite, even restricted, does not exist in our physical world. Constructed and used for your geometry, the infinite can be as you wish; your line may contain an uncountable number of points. But the number of dots in any line which is a thing in our world can only be finite and countable. Each can have a name, although silly to assign one.

EUCLID: Now that the gods suggest it, the finiteness and discreteness of the things of the world seems obvious. Objects are somehow kept apart from each other. But I had not considered that there might be a difference from my constructs!

PLATO: To be a thing in our world, a point cannot be infinitely small, but only very, very small. It does not matter how these tiny pieces come to be or how they interact. The lines and points of your geometry cannot be physical lines and points. As construct within your mind, no worldly example exists, only your description. If anything infinitely large existed, it would swallow up and subsume everything else within its limitlessness.

EUCLID: Such a result, being foreign to the way we have been taught to think about things, is hard to accept. The gods say that the finiteness of our world is a reality. And, as I said, it does seem obvious. Worldly examples must be separate from my geometry, and from my ellipse itself. It seems that my question is answered.

The habits of our minds

PLATO: Not quite so fast, my friend. First you must decide whether the ellipse you refer to is a construct within your mind, a geometry or mental model perhaps, or instead, a thing in the real world. It could readily be either. But not both at once. If simply a construct in your mind, having the general shape of the ellipse you have drawn, then it could readily contain a number of points beyond counting, or whatever you like. But if you decide it to be a thing in the real world, with an itself-by-itself and a Form via its name, then its number of 'points' must be finite.   It doesn't matter a whit how small the points are nor how many they be; a number for them does indeed exist.

Object or construct?

EUCLID: How simple you make it sound.

PLATO: But that is not all. If a thing of the world, your ellipse has these points only inside itself. Something keeps them together, an identifiable if movable boundary. A construct can be as you wish, its boundary being one of pure description and visualization.

EUCLID: It may sound simple, but you do manage to keep my mind churning.

PLATO: Beyond those two matters, if your ellipse is one of the real world, its weight must also have measure, no matter how you decide to measure it. On the other hand, as a construct in your mind or as a geometric model, its weight would have neither measure nor import.

EUCLID: I do understand your distinction, philosopher or not.

*Paradigms
of thought*

PLATO: The Soul can gain value from things of the world with their Forms, but also from constructs of the mind.   The two seem to be the same because we have been taught to think in such a way, but the construct is not a thing of the world. If we wish to discuss an ellipse, we must be clear about the subject of our discussion.   The three things, being the construct in my mind, the construct in your mind or the thing of the world, are distinct.   Nor can the name we put on any of the three be its itself-by-itself. An elusive difficulty.

EUCLID: There seems to be a gap, starting with the one between objects and names. I am the one who placed a name on both ellipses, considering them to be one, and unaware that it mattered which type I was naming. And it had seemed so clear.

PLATO: You have no reason to know of it, but I discussed these gaps at length some time ago with Solomon of Jerusalem.

EUCLID: There is also a gap between mind and matter of a different kind. Constructs of the mind have a different kind of existence from seemingly similar things of the world, no matter which ellipse they model, and separate from the names we have been discussing.   One really needs clarity for right opinion, and tethering to pin the matter down!

Dimensionality

PLATO: Tethering is your specialty, so I'll leave that for you.   But there is more. The gods also suggested to me that, for our actual world such an ellipse might serve as a useful model for, as they put it, a *'curvature of space-time dimensionality.'*   They put those strange-sounding words on what we see as the dimensions of space and time (three from your geometry), using those words to describe the entirety of the world we live in. Constructs to be sure, but we are bounded by our minds even as we try to cast our gaze beyond.

EUCLID: Such fancy words go beyond my own poor ability. But I think that you intend a simple description for a complicated idea. I never really considered time as a dimension.

PLATO: Words of the gods. We know objects, but do not think of them apart from a presence in space. We know of movement or action, but cannot describe motion without using time. Even though your ellipse has but two dimensions, it is an easy piece for us to imagine extending the notion.

Motion is elusive

EUCLID: It might well be useful to help understand complex matters.

PLATO: The gods also disclosed to me this: in the space-time curvature, all things, which are finite and countable in number, are also continually in motion.

EUCLID: Now that you mention it, I can see that those two aspects of things or objects are indeed what we observe.

PLATO: Strange as it may seem to us who think we see a rock sitting quietly, at rest and unmoving, one cannot know the true location and the speed of such a thing at any moment in time, so it must be in motion. It becomes elusive to clarify, both to separate the infinite from the finite, and also, to truly pin down the nature of a thing. But we must see the matter clearly; our world is finite, with the infinite only a useful construct for your geometry, enabling description. There is much confusion because we use words as is convenient in the moment, rather than staying faithful to a single meaning.

The convenience of words

EUCLID: I do not see how that changes the result for my ellipse?

PLATO: Indeed it does not; two kinds of ellipse remain. Let us consider the case of a real-world ellipse, particularly the one which represents the totality of the world itself. If we consider its Form, the itself-by-itself, a finite thing, there are still gaps between each of the parts which make it up. We know there are parts because our world consists of objects in motion; the parts must be

The world as a totality

separated or there could be no parts. The parts of the real-world ellipse can see each other but cannot see outside of that world. There can be no perceivable 'outside.' Otherwise, the ellipse would not be a totality.

EUCLID: What you say makes sense. How about the other?

PLATO: An ellipse as useful construct is completely filled with points. An infinite number of points or else it would not satisfy any of the rules of your geometry. The similarity to the other physical ellipse is simply because we say so. You and I may see the matter differently. We may also find and agree upon countless predictive rules that apply equally well for both. But it seems likely that

Models are imperfect

we will have to continually modify the rules of the one to have them work for the other, reminding us that the one has reality as a thing of the world; the other does not, being construct. These two ellipses are much the same as shadows versus real objects, a matter discussed by Socrates and Glaucon. The relationship between the constructed picture and the object we truly wish to study and know is elusive at best.

EUCLID: From what the gods have told you as true, both seem right opinion. If I am in and part of such a world of things, I cannot see what is not in it. The finite cannot reach out and touch the infinite. If it could, it would itself have to be infinite.

PLATO: A final question may occur to you, dear Euclid, one where I have come to a different view from what I once believed. Where does the infinite, which must even include the gods themselves, truly reside? Not in our world, since the location itself must be infinite in all ways. Being such, and seeing from such a location, all that we know and see and experience, would be the merest speck, both time and space collapsed into essential nothingness. Such is mere speculation, but seems right opinion.

Location and role of the gods?

EUCLID: You take my mind in interesting directions.

PLATO: As with all such matters, we cannot know or discover the answer. Perhaps the place is in another dimension, or in the space outside your ellipse and outside of our space-time world, or in the gaps between the things inside. Looking from such a seat, seeing the ellipse and our finite world as a bunch of things, how easy for the gods to reach out with a common thumb, to squash or twirl or nudge, all or any part, on whim or by choice. Being infinite, the occupier of that seat could reach inside all of the objects or the spaces between them, touching anything without any ability for the finite things inside to perceive either the actions or the touch. Such touching could even include ourselves, in any manner whatever, without any ability for us to touch back or to perceive.

EUCLID: Since I am used to constructs of the mind, even though I did not recognize them to be such before this conversation, the leap is not so great.

PLATO: To us, such a power must be unperceived because it is outside our space-time curvature. But to such gods, your ellipse and our world are so very small indeed. All our dimensions of space and time, the totality of all of our things, now and our forever, is the tiniest speck. The infinite encompasses a true 'all' including anything finite. By definition, there is nothing outside. That seems to mean only one 'god' is possible, with our finite just a tiny blip inside of the one infinite. Perhaps even many tiny finites!

EUCLID: All of this the gods revealed to you?

Three truths from the gods

PLATO: Oh no. Only three things, all of whose truth seems compelling: an inescapable and definitional understanding for the infinite, outside of which nothing can lie; the existence of a space-time curvature with finiteness for our world; and the impossibility for us to identify the location and velocity of any thing of our world at one moment. All of the rest, and even those three, I put forward to you for tethering as right opinion.

EUCLID: I am so pleased to have met you here on these streets.

PLATO: Equally so for me, but now I must hurry off. I have such a bad habit of being late.

JOHN: And so they parted. An interesting and enlightening conversation, don't you think, dear Sarah? I don't believe they ever met again. Athens and Alexandria are a long way apart, and Plato did not seem to travel much.

Conjecture as a pathway to truth

SARAH: Those thoughts coincide so readily with my reading of last night, prompted by these same concerns, instructive reading for a learner such as myself. How nicely Plato summed up the nature of "conjecture" as we currently use the word.

JOHN: As simple students, best that we both stay away from what would likely turn into an endless debate over truth versus conjecture.

SARAH: In *A Brief History of Time*, S.A. Hawking refers to his proof of the finiteness of the universe, a bounded space-time curvature. But such an idea is a very great extension from the simple version cited by Plato. Hawking and others clarify, that their meaning is a fixed sum total of all of the matter and energy in the universe, recognizing constant on-going interchangeability between what we label as matter and what we call energy. Nonetheless, the simple version serves, with the shadow of $E = mc^2$ not changing the essence of finiteness and countability. The interchangeability of matter and energy is crucial to understanding the itself-by-itself for the objects of the world, but not so much for its finiteness and countability. Nor do our human limitations for "visibility" impact "observability." We can readily accept what we now call "dark" forms of matter and energy. Our limited ability to observe only in particular ways does not limit our ability to perceive in other ways, nor does either limitation affect the finiteness and countability of the world.

Matter, energy and perception

JOHN: Another point well made.

SARAH: We should discuss the words of the gods which came to Plato so many years ago. Simple, yet not. Let us remember to be clear without straying into constructs and excess words.

JOHN: You will have to explain.

SARAH: Hawking's finiteness is of boundedness, relating to the very large. As such, it needs no further clarity, even if the picture of an ellipse may distract us from an actual appearance.

JOHN: With the omni-present interchangeability of matter and energy, visualization of the nature of any boundary would seem elusive. But images are always helpful for my poor mind.

SARAH: What affects the outcome is that any mathematical proof of his type would require a

Boundedness, continuity and connectedness

continuous geometry. Continuity consists of adding an infinite number of the infinitely small to what might otherwise be a discrete and discontinuous set, as in our case. Being bounded, such a set will remain countable, a characteristic unchanged by adding any number of the infinitely small. When it merely serves a proof which is based on constructs, it is of no consequence for our discussion about the real world. Since our world is finite, it simply cannot encompass the infinite, except in this trivial and meaningless sense of the infinitely small. Adding points, having location but without extension, does not change the fundamental reality of a countable (and finite) set. Everything of substance to do with the infinite, being the large, is purely a construct of our minds.

JOHN: I think I am seeing your picture of the infinite, a most convincing one. A countable infinite is excluded in your usage.

Constructs and the abstract

SARAH: Perhaps it would be good to clarify our understanding of other words we use. The words, *"constructs of our mind,"* has come up many times. We could also describe such as the products which arise from the human capability for abstract thinking and for expressing abstract thoughts. 'Ideas' might be a reasonable substitute. Both seem to be uniquely human. Perhaps the existence of constructs or ideas is even the feature that best describes "human-ness."

JOHN: Otherwise, we would not be here talking to each other!

SARAH: Also, there must be at least two of us for thoughts and conversation to have any reality or utility. We have proceeded happily along in our conversations without stating the necessary, that our conversations themselves are pure abstractions, about things of the world to be sure, but also about the concepts themselves. We must deal in constructs.

JOHN: Humans and communication. That necessity occurred to me when you first described a "point." Dearly as I love my dog, he could not understand nor express such a concept. He cannot take what he sees or feels or senses, then make it abstract, into something separate. Nor can he go on to express ideas about it.

SARAH: Or number. A construct as well, as our friend Plato came to realize when he accepted the tree-ness of each tree, and the separateness of Forms, with each object a separate "one." Objects are collectively countable and finite because countability is a useful construct for sharing ideas, as well as being a necessary fact about the world. There is no "two" in the real world. Countability and all of mathematics including numbers form a language, a language just as surely as our words, all designed to help us to be clear about our abstractions. But with clarity come the limitations imposed by a consequent need for precise rules, a need we can avoid by focusing on the objects of the real world. As humans, we like rules. As conversationalists, we need them, even as we quickly forget to stick to them.

There is no "two"

JOHN: Yes, we are interested in knowing about things of the world, not constructs. If there are no "two's," there really aren't any "one's" either, just the each-ness of each thing of the world. Countability and separation lead to inevitable uniqueness. How abstractions do ensnare us, but enrich us just as surely. Our minds are the most useful tool we have.

SARAH: Well said. All things being finite and countable does give clarity about our world, as well as a certain kind of simplicity.

JOHN: You know that Plato at one time would have rejected any connection between the gods and the infinite. The infinite contains every imperfection in the world, a world which he wished to uncover as perfect. No matter, since Hawking and others have given us these well-tethered hypotheses. The passage of time creates awkward bedfellows. At an earlier date, Heisenberg and others gave us hypotheses about the uncertainty principle which are now well-tethered. How wonderful is the mind of man to gradually clarify these matters.

The infinite

SARAH: There is other import to what was said. As a construct of the mind, it is easy to construct not just one infinite, but many. Each line can have infinite extension in one or both directions. But looked at more accurately, there can only be one actual infinite, with its nature unknown and unknowable. Everything, including the world which we can perceive, is inside it; nothing outside. The truly infinitesimal does not affect that reality.

JOHN: Quite so.

SARAH: If dimension restricts the world, it cannot mean what we claim for it. For the world itself, only objects and motion are real. Constructs can assist our vision and understanding, but are separate matters, subject to additional created rules. We must also be clear when we speak, and carefully choose our 'infinite.'

The elusiveness of "all"

JOHN: I see the makings of a potential problem. We are wont to divide objects or arguments or all manner of choices into two classes. There are objects which are white, so we say that all remaining objects are not white. But which "all" do we mean: the infinite "all" or the finite, countable one? If we think we mean an infinite "all," then we describe and classify something about which we cannot know anything. A true existence for the infinite, even as a part of our way of thinking, would seem to make a mess of any argumentation which is based on a simple choice between 'true' and 'not true.' Even early philosophers recognized this difficulty, reducing it to a matter of perspective. From our vantage point, "true" and "not true" make sense. From the perspective of the infinite, they do not, because everything is encompassed in a one: true and untrue, known and unknowable.

SARAH: A face for another problem as well, but with a helpful way out. Our perpetual dilemma with discovering truth is the problem of our vantage point, or as Euclid pointed out, the inescapable gap between mind and matter, subject and object. But the ever-presence of the third class, the unknowable, allows us to honestly bounce back and forth, a continuum of seeing objects both in themselves and for themselves, thesis and antithesis, a merging of every matter with its ever-present negation, even if unknowable from a starting vantage point.

The unknowable

JOHN: With those thoughts, you remind me of G.W.F. Hegel, also unaware of the same three "matters from the gods" as stated by Plato. Consider his book *Phenomenology of Spirit*. His amazing deconstruction/reconstruction of our mind's search for truth seems no more nor less than how we or our mind must 'manage the gap' between mind and matter, allowing for the unknowable. A universality of process, not result. Not surprisingly, he ends up with a place or process or thing he calls Spirit as his final management tool. Perhaps we may end up in a similar quandary.

SARAH: Indeed, and it is a very skillfully described sequence. It is also an excellent description of a quality control process at work, likely a good description the way our minds have advanced since we were first able to process observations, as babies or as humans. The process corrects itself by sensing the flaws of the current process, the unknowable, adjusting to overload with

Quality control

negation and simplification, moving on to include ever more perceptions and constructs.

JOHN: A good description of quality control.

SARAH: But let's go back. In addition to the crucial distinction between a model or construct versus a thing of the world, the discussion between Euclid and Plato has clarified the matter you raised last night.

JOHN: How so?

The endless sequence of naming

SARAH: Your question was "where does it end?" referring to the naming of things, with an apparently limitless sequence of names and Forms. It is now clear that we do not need to know, nor perhaps can we know or even visualize, where it ends because of the use of constructs. Every object in the world exists, with mass and observability. Not so for constructs which often start as names. With finite countability for the totality after those names are made into objects, the sequence must end. Our mind is inescapably intertwined with our abstractions. But once we convert constructs into real objects, the rules for those objects apply.

JOHN: That is a fact we cannot escape. There is also the role of ourselves as observers that limits our understanding.

Objectifying constructs

SARAH: Most likely the sequence doesn't even start. A mathematician or logician answers such questions by creating a construct, a model. When we too assign a name, we create a construct, whether aware of it or not. But we remain unable to make our model itself into a thing in the world, only the created name or picture for it. In answering your question, we must be clear about our use of constructs in formulating or clarifying. If so, what is their true nature? Among things of the world, it seems hard to find any natural sequencing or ordering such as found in your transition from objects to constructs. No hierarchy.

JOHN: You have identified both the problem and its answer. Constructs, such as dimensionality, have become how we now see and talk about the world, rather than seeing only the objects and their motion. Your face tells me that you have more to say, although we need to come back later to more depth on these matters.

SARAH: I always have more to say. As for Plato, perhaps it is still too early to know where his ever-active mind might have ended up. Or mine as well. It was not for nothing that I studied mathematics, even if as an amateur. Before I venture there, let me make another matter clear. I hope we both understand that when we hear the ancients talk of what the gods told them, we are only to understand that the source or truth of the information could not then be identified, that what we might call a *deus ex machina* was at work. Facts are facts, whether or not we know them. Thanks to Hawking, Heisenberg and others, we now know the identities of those *dei*, and can know facts not yet available to the ancients. When the ancients, and ourselves in these conversations, use the word 'world' or 'real world,' we really intend and understand the word 'universe' as we understand and use the latter word today.

Clarification of terminology

JOHN: A good idea to state the clarifications, but I think that the matter was clear.

SARAH: An interesting property that is held by any collection of things which is finite, such as the space-time curvature of our universe, is that it is mappable or projectable onto a finite set (or collection) of any other shape or dimensionality, even to a one-dimensional space such as a line. Only the countability of the two spaces must be the same, or the latter larger. If both finite spaces have the same countability and if the proper information

Geometries

is transferred in the mapping, then the projection can be completely reversed, re-creating the original collection down to its tiniest detail.

JOHN: Does that take us anywhere?

SARAH: Perhaps. It can help us understand that the construct which is our geometry need have no real substance, only rules. Nor does any particular geometry merit the total reliance we have come to place upon it. It seems to me also, that, in thinking of such things, one ought to exclude the dimension of time and allow it to be a special case.

Time

JOHN: You are going to have to lead me by the hand.

SARAH: From our human point of view, time is a singularity, pure and simple, a 'Now.' In his *Confessions*, Augustine gave a most lucid explanation, as he also did for aspects of the infinite which we discussed earlier. But he failed to reduce either to its nature as construct, thereby leading himself into a dead-end. Time seems necessary as a construct in order that we can describe motion which is itself existential, independent of us as humans with our constructs. But the reality of time is a singularity, being simply the current moment. We cannot perceive before or after the current moment. Such is our world of only objects and motion, the simplest and most self-evident premise. We use time in a manner which identifies its boundedness in the past; our premises require that our world came into being. The course of time in the future is of no consequence and definitively outside of the realm of possible observation. Time is useful, but hollow. Being a singularity in reality, even if not so as construct, the question of dimensionality or continuity for time is irrelevant. Constructs are as we wish them to be; if continuity for time is useful for calculations, so be it.

Persistence vs existence

JOHN: Are you saying that existence and persistence must be separate things?

SARAH: The latter, as we mostly use it, is indeed simply a construct, a child of time. Both come to us through our ability to think abstractly. Motion exists, so we wish to have a way to talk about it. More than that, since time is a singularity, persistence becomes a necessary construct for us to perceive the fact of motion, but a separate construct for each observer. The dimension of time has become our useful shorthand for these efforts. As construct, time can behave as we wish. My perception of motion is through the construct of persistence which has thereby acquired the same reality as if it actually exists as more than a convenience for our use!

JOHN: Such things do easily become part of what we think of as our world.

SARAH: Let us go back to the projection or mapping. As long as one posits an infinite number of the infinitely small between each thing in both spaces, then continuity in either space does not affect the outcome either. Who then is even to say what is the true dimensionality of our space-time curvature? Three for Space and one for Time seems merely a convenient method chosen by our geometers. It matters not. Your earlier question disappears, in part because the succession, as in many similar paradoxes, has time as an integral component.

Choices of convenience

JOHN: That seems a well-reasoned observation. Objects and motion, with the latter dependent on the former for existence, I hear you say. Time is our own child from both, as are constructs. As a singularity, time is neither object nor construct.

SARAH: That captures the thought. How ironic that moderns have so quickly discarded their requirement that the simple linear geometry of Euclid be a true feature of the world, even as construct. It is locally useful, but does not accurately represent the true time-space curvature. The irony arises because the same moderns are unwilling to deal similarly with time. Since there is only a Now, whether we choose to think of what we call 'time' as linear, either locally or globally, makes no difference. We cannot devise experiments to otherwise know anything about a reality for 'time' in any case. So the geometry we choose to represent it is for our own convenience, as a way to make calculations and deal with persistence. The fact of only a Now is a fact. We can only sense time through the existence of motion. Objects and motion, or change if your prefer. Both seem to be perceived at some level by everything we consider to have alive-ness, even things unable to say so.

JOHN: You do like to take matters in interesting directions!

Details about objects

SARAH: Likewise, it matters not whether what we call an "object" is a single one or in fact contains thousands of smaller bits. We know of the boundedness on largeness, but smallness is less consequential. Finite countability is the essence. Whether what we now call a small particle eventually proves to dissolve into ever smaller particles, or even into discrete force and energy fields, matters not. A limit to smallness is helpful for separation, but of no real import to the nature of the world. Countability, discreteness, location and movement remain as the essence.

JOHN: You surprise me at times with your descriptions.

Limitations of dimensionality

SARAH: Before we part, let me tell you of two other readings. I have tried to study these matters from several points of view. *Flatland* by E.A. Abbott, despite its flaws, is a simple picture of the inability of things in one dimensionality to "see" anything outside of that dimensionality, perhaps better stated as the ability to see only what amounts to a single edge or shadow of that 'anything.' His focus is narrower than what I heard you relate from Plato and Euclid, but the book is an easy piece, and useful nonetheless.

JOHN: I do recall its brevity.

SARAH: In *Mere Christianity*, C.S. Lewis raises the question of where gods might sit and how they might behave, stopping a bit short of where you and I have gone today. Science had not then evolved as it has since, with matters from the gods still elusive.

JOHN: Isn't it helpful that each new conversation can probe matters from a different, and perhaps even new, point of view? Perhaps un-covery rather than discovery?

SARAH: Best to stop. It would be hard to list and do justice to all of the glimpses by other writers in science and theology. Most of the wisps just seem to blur the vision.

JOHN: We have resolved two matters leading directly into elusive gaps. You and I talked about them yesterday. There is an unbridgeable gap between the name or description of a thing and the thing or its Form itself, a mind-to-matter gap. And the separateness of things of the world from our models or mental constructs, even ones purported to represent those things, is clear-cut but unbridgeable, a matter-to-mind gap, another trap for our thinking and discussions. Both results seem well-tethered after our discussions, and necessarily real from what we know of our world. These gaps are identifiable and we can perceive precisely where they lie.

Elusive gaps

SARAH: If one sees no utility or necessity to exploring these gaps, Plato's final question about the residence of the gods has no meaning. The gaps are identified by observation, but cannot be bridged by science through no fault of its own. Even those who choose to hide their eyes must accept the finiteness of the world. It is physical scope of what we all seek to explore and know.

JOHN: It is a finiteness so large that its bounds will never be a practical limit for science.

The ematomic is a "gossamer curtain of steel"

SARAH: For clarity, I like the thought of a gossamer curtain of steel to describe these gaps between mind and matter, also to include matter-to-matter, with Heisenberg uncertainty. So filmy and thin as to seem irrelevant, yet impenetrable. Mind and matter. They seem not so much gaps as barriers to knowledge, or walls. Perhaps different wording will be useful. I shall call them the "*ematomic.*" Such a word suggests an atomic emptiness. Let them be ematomic gaps, collectively constituting an ematomic wall. Each class of these gaps is finite, because matter consists of a finite number of objects, and thereby countable), as are the number of discrete and living minds. Their intersection is finite.

Naming objects is helpful

JOHN: Words often seem poor servants, but it is good to put a word on these elusive "absences." It is very hard to discuss things which are not named. But are you sure there is substantial difference between some of the ematomic gaps you have described? They seem much the same.

Details about the ematomic

SARAH: I see your point. And I had forgotten what I said earlier about matter-to-matter gaps. Discreteness, countability, those account for the matter-to-matter gaps and take them into the finite, but they are still elusive. Expressing or naming an abstraction creates an object, mind-to-matter. Matter-to-mind goes in the other direction by naming an itself-by-itself. But both use constructs. But they show that there is a reality to explore even though is actually unbridgeable gap, a certain kind of nothingness. The other matter, that an expressed construct must have a name, is distinct from its presence inside our mind as construct. The expression of it objectifies the construct. All gaps are part of the ematomic wall or entirety, so the distinctions do not really matter.

JOHN: That is just what I was thinking. Perhaps it is best to leave aside the space between things of the world which seems to be not as invisible to science as the ematomic. Objects do have space between them, but possibly that vacuum may come to be explored by science.

SARAH: If we omit the matter-to-matter gaps, the choice of mind-to-matter or matter-to-mind also seems irrelevant. A gap is just a missing piece, having no need of directionality. A name as a construct of the mind is definitively not the thing in itself, the itself-by-itself. Let the word "dog" be a construct, alongside an ellipse, with or without its pixels. It is not the dog itself.

JOHN: I agree.

SARAH: Aside from the gaps, there is other relevance in the essence of a construct versus that of an object, but that would take us astray. Avicenna wrote lucidly about essence versus existence, although in doing so, he dealt exclusively with constructs. He ignored the ematomic as well. The existence of these gaps is the heart of the matter. It has either been ignored, or by-passed using by every philosopher throughout history, many falling into the same trap as Avicenna by relying on constructs

Ematomic dilemmas in philosophy

JOHN: The ematomic seems clear to me for these instances.

SARAH: If we were to uncover a mind-to-mind gap, might not our picture be even more complete? Are you starting to fidget, doubtless over another point you would like to make?

JOHN: With that extra moment you just gave me, I can see that my other question is already answered. Even as mind can apparently change to matter, as at death, and perhaps at more indeterminate times, only the category and focus for the ematomic gap would change, with the words 'mind' and 'matter' changing places. A type-A ematomic gap becomes a type-B ematomic gap. These gaps are so elusive.

Science and the gaps

SARAH: Furthermore, whether we can discover things about the gaps themselves between objects, the matter-to-matter gaps, makes no real difference. I would prefer to leave these gaps, or voids as science might call them, outside of my definition of ematomic gaps for the sake of clarity. They remain countable since there is one and only one gap between each pair of objects. They are potentially subject to the same study by science as objects themselves. Let us just call these "voids," or if it better serves, the singular word "void" for their entirety since it seems clear that they must be contiguous.

JOHN: Your intention seems good, but science may take matters in another direction by exploring each one as a different kind of object in its own right.

SARAH: I think not. But since you make the point, if you prefer, we can still include them as ematomic. We cannot evade the important parts of the ematomic wall which are not these. While many things have been examined by inference, such study as I have seen is a study of constructs, not objects, and is itself a constructed method. The possibility of direct study of an absence rather a presence is hard to imagine.

JOHN: Such speculation seems merely a diversion from our pursuit, although one that Euclid would have readily understood.

SARAH: Quite true. All consequences and impacts from the existence of the gaps would remain untouched. If time is merely a Now, any difficulty in the scrutiny of matter itself, due to its interchangeability with energy and the uncertainty as to its location, remains irrelevant for study of the ematomic wall. The wall arises from the distinction between constructs and objects, with the need of names arising from the necessity of observers.

The world is nonsensical without the ematomic

JOHN: Your mind races ahead. I sense no desire in you to rest, so have success in your search, wherever it leads. I do have some thoughts for another day, but only one more for today. If a gap between mind and matter did not exist, what would remain?

SARAH: That question seems couched in the language of a proof by contradiction, a powerful method of proof.

JOHN: We would be left with either a world of rocks and trees and mice, with no humans to attach names to such things, or a world of floating names, pure minds with nothing for them to describe. Both alternatives make nonsense of everything we experience. And of our ability to experience it. And of any reason for participation. Either pure being, with no one to know that "being" is a possibility, or else pure "ability-to-know," with nothing to sense or be known. Non-human animates or in-animates, hats and cats which simply react to happenings or other objects, lacking the ability to describe.

Proof

SARAH: Such is the contradiction which arises if either alternative reality were true. Either objects without observer, or observers without objects to observe. You have certainly helped me to clarify the necessary existence of the ematomic gaps, the wall.

JOHN: And what a delight to discuss these matters and to receive instruction with you. So few are the pleasures remaining for a well-worn mind and body.

SARAH: You are the one guilty of giving both the pleasure and the instruction. Conversation and mutual exploration benefits me greatly. A toast to tomorrow?

Sarah's Search

Being One Terminus for the Conversations

SARAH: Dear John, good morning yet again. I am so excited. Let me relate to you a conversation I had after parting with you yesterday. It was with Plato himself.

JOHN: A moment, please. Our discussion might be better served if I first recounted the words I overheard, so that both of us could better test our minds.

SARAH: Oh, you scoundrel!

JOHN: Not so; merely the method of a tireless observer. The conversation was thus:

PLATO: My friend John told me a while ago that you might beSarah and might wish to meet with me. It is a surprise to see you out so late. He told me to expect a treat.

SARAH: That is high praise indeed as John has great insight and many talents. I did not know you knew him?

PLATO: He seems ageless to me, and knows more than I as well.

SARAH: He has a way of being in more places than one might suppose. To fill you in, my teachers, andJohn is one, suggested that perhaps a meeting with Plato might be of value for my education. And even more, for the good health of my Soul, as they put it. John told me of your three messages from the gods. It occurs to me that perhaps your Forms are not now quite as restricted as once appeared from your early thinking? As I hear it told, the matters of the infinite cannot be encompassed or

Elusiveness redux

constricted by earthly things, since they must have the freedom of the unbounded. Can you explain these matters to me in your own words?

Objects vs constructs

PLATO: Let us see where matters take us. As we go forward to explore, we must always be vigilant as to whether we speak of a thing of the world, and in what way. If we speak of a thing of the world, it can be identified and named and has a Form. It exists and has an itself-by-itself, but is elusive as to its nature because it cannot be fully pinned down. It may not appear the same for the two of us, nor even for each of us alone at two different moments. But it has a reality nonetheless.

SARAH: I believe that your earlier conversation with Euclid of Alexandria showed how constructs can also become things of the world.

PLATO: Any idea in my mind, when it takes shape as expression, then becomes a finite thing of the world, even if still in my mind or expressed to others. Its content remains construct; its form, a real thing, an object. The content need have no bounds. It has no necessary relationship to any other thing of the world, and is purely as we make it. In the process of creating and using the Form as a real thing, we easily lose sight of its origin as construct. Unconsciously and unintentionally.

SARAH: While unavoidable as reality, it is equally unavoidable that we must converse as we are doing now. What irony! To learn about some matter which has no bounds, such as the infinite, we must use constructs we have created. A dilemma.

PLATO: We can and do imagine infinity in many ways, and build mathematics upon it, neither being things of the world. Just as surely, I can tell you of what is in my mind, but I cannot actually put it into your mind and have it be the same. Our two minds remain separate, joined only by conversation. Even as I remember a conversation, I translate it into an expression of my own, no matter how lengthy, nor whether doing so consciously or unconsciously. Our expressions are themselves things, but mine are not yours. Nor yours, mine. At least not until untethered from me.

SARAH: Nearly everyone must have noted that separation, but likely without saying so. You may not know a fellow lover of knowledge named Augustine. That realization of the separateness of humans, one from another, led him to re-think his entire life and purpose. For others, the realization, if it happened, might have been more subconscious, and seldom a matter for serious reflection. Far too obvious to be noted!

Making the obvious obvious

PLATO: For me, I don't recall giving the matter much thought, but I may have. It seems natural and obvious and unavoidable. Our two minds are indeed fully separate. But I can also see that others might not have sensed the nature and implications of the separateness.

SARAH: There is nothing either of us can do about that reality. Even if I could transplant an expression, it would no longer be mine, under my control. If I am "on the same wave-length" as you, thoughts may indeed be transmitted but only between the two of us in an instant, the transmitter then losing control. An expression may become an object in motion, but its content as construct has the bounds of one specific imagination. This gift of the gods, in forming a manner of separation of our world from the infinite, creates enduring dialogue. It gives us passion for exploration and a pleasure to our souls from philosophy, trying to describe the Forms, and perhaps even reasons for the pleasure of the exploration. Each phrase we utter, each sentence we read, comes strictly from the mind of the utterer, having no necessary tie to reality. My mind is mine; your mind is yours.

Individual-ness

PLATO: You make the case quite clearly. With joy and vigor, we can examine the world, just as craftsmen do, or

Inquisitiveness

simply as observers and users of things. We can also examine the achievements of the craftsmen as they show and talk about their craft and their wares. Each thing observed opens great numbers of new Forms for us, inside and outside the mind of the observer. Just as surely, we are driven to explore such endless bounty, disregarding that, for final clarity, it may well seem to take us to where the infinite and the unknowable reside. Seeking things which we know that we cannot fully understand seems circular. But it still burns us with a fire of unquenchable passion.

SARAH: Such a quest seems to be what I hear and find with Love: the more of it that I give, the more of it which remains inside of me still to be given. Unquenchable. By the limits in our ability to have knowledge, whether by ourselves or in communion, the appetite for it is whetted! But it leads us to overlook some realities which limit us.

PLATO: Spoken as a true scholar.

Finiteness

SARAH: Separately, the infinite gods, being infinite, must have kept for themselves the power to touch us or tell us or force us, with us helpless to know with certainty whether or not we have been so touched or told or forced. The finite reality of our world leads many places, but keeps us apart from others. As does the footnote of the gods that, in the ordinary course of time, the stuff of which all things are made is neither created nor destroyed as we would understand those words, no matter how it moves about. The sum total remains fixed, and further proof that the content of our expressions is not a thing of the world.

PLATO: That is somewhat as I had supposed from what Phaedo told me about Soul and body, but it remained unclear.

SARAH: I understand such a thing from scientific inquiry, with the word "conjecture" now in common use. But please explain.

PLATO: Let me start with Phaedo relating to me Socrates' words, that all learning in our world must be recollection. I now think that idea falls short: it is only the elemental stuff of things which remains permanent. Most actual things, whether past, present or future, can and must be recombinations of the elemental stuff. What I had supposed to be 'recollection' might be a recombination, not the previous thing itself. A 'created' new idea. And while unnecessary for the result, who is to say that a creation or destruction, no matter how infrequent or how unlikely, has not occurred? The creations and the destructions cannot be infinite either, since everything stays inside the world and remains part of the finite and countable things of the world.

Creation and destruction

SARAH: Learning might be much the same as architecture, taking pieces of what exists and putting them together in another way. Perhaps even a totally new way?

PLATO: A good objective for all education. Indeed, education, with perception, and conversation are the only means we have to actually expand the collection of constructs that our minds can use. But the inspiration and the driving force and the creativity to put that stuff together must also occur within the mind, perhaps of one person, perhaps of many. That is where I would now study. It does not seem to come directly from parents, by way of inheritance as you would call it, not even for craftsmen, whether explorers or molders. How seldom do the inspired and the creative come from inspired parents! The gift of inspiration falls instead to those with time and opportunity to use their minds, possibly with luck as well. Parents may indeed foster the opportunities.

How does the mind work?

Repetition?

SARAH: You know, dear teacher Plato, I think you are right. My grandfather told me once of some wisdom that he had heard from his grandfather, namely that we cannot repeat any experience with exactitude if for no other reason than that the attempt itself at repeat must always be influenced in some way by knowledge of the previous experience, a persistence which happens for us inside our minds. Usually it drives men to improve, however slightly, a previous effort. We seldom wish to precisely repeat, even if we say that we are trying to do so.

PLATO: The mind is ever at work. Never mind that craftsmen claim that identical replication is possible, indeed strive for it. But does that thought answer for the source of the inspiration?

SARAH: My great-great-grandfather spoke of wishes and sensations, as well as experiences. As matters of one's own self, as constructs, none of those can be replicated in any other self. So if those matters have any commonalty for us all, being similar or even the same in the chosen words of description by others, despite constantly changing instances, the source for them must come from elsewhere.

Education

PLATO: In the matter of a tree, as a thought given to me by Solomon of Jerusalem some time ago, the varying instances seem to cause no problem. For the content of the mind, our constructs which encompass the infinite and necessarily create unanswerable questions, it does not serve. We have a dilemma. Each of us is surrounded by our own collection of things, whether ideas, possessions, attributes or expressions. How is it that we unite our being with others, indeed that we can have any conversation with another in a way that allows us to understand in any way what the other is saying or seeing? When face-to-face as you and I, our other senses such as sight and hearing impact even the meaning of the chosen words. Our ideas are separate and distinct from those of another, so how does any commonalty arise? Conversations are the only avenue.

SARAH: Now you come to the heart of a perplexing matter. Is it possible for the world to have put itself into the kind of whole we see, with us as beings asking the kinds of questions we ask, throughout all recorded time, in all recorded cultures, and by every manner of humankind, including questions about the infinite, without the infinite itself existing? Since we cannot experience the infinite, which is not a part of the world, from where can that idea have come to us? Such thoughts prompt me to move from science into speculation.

PLATO: For myself, striving to be a pure thinker, I focus on truth. But my mind does go in other directions, so not all truth may be knowable truth. Speculation will be fun. Perhaps we shall learn.

SARAH: Indeed. Much from history is known. The earliest writings are simply descriptions of what was seen and what was happening, done by means of pictures, not written language, with no evidence of an ability to think abstractly. The first known evidence of a human ability to create constructs was a written list of the laws necessary for people to live together, assembled by Hammurabi in Mesopotamia many years before your time. But that date is only a tiny blip in the totality of time if one considers the lifespan of a rock!

PLATO: A dog can only tell us about the bone in front of him, or not. Not so for humans. Our own minds go everywhere.

SARAH: The first urgency of writers was not current events nor happenings, but practical constructs. As thought evolved into greater ability than managing the needs of the moment, humans immediately went to the matters that we have considered here, about origins and about how we came to be as we are, with a sense that something greater than what we see around us had a hand in making it happen. Once an ability to create constructs appeared, very early thinking was about the Form of existence itself, a matter we cannot know because it is outside of our Now. The earliest constructs of men either served as laws for collective management needs, or dwelt on matters which could never have been directly observed!

Early records of constructs

PLATO: I see your point precisely. Whenever I raised a matter for study, it dealt with something I saw or felt or perceived, passing quickly and unconsciously from objects in front of me to matters inside my mind, one of which might have been a concept of the infinite. Equally unconsciously, I sought some kind of evidence for the existence of a Form, grasping at what I see now was purely inside my mind. Now that this matter of the infinite and the inescapable gaps to knowing have come so clearly into focus, how can one say other than that the infinite most likely does exist. But it must be outside our world of things. Unknowable, yes, but we do not immediately know that something is unknowable and not a part of the things of the world. The idea for it must have come from somewhere.

SARAH: When one sees the evolving power of constructs of the mind such as mathematics, whose grounding and usefulness in the world comes in part from adding the idea of the infinite to the world we see, how can one doubt that what you say is right opinion? The record shows that an idea of an infinite, beyond and outside us, came into being at almost the same time as the very first evidence that our minds could have ideas. Mathematics came later, to help show how the infinite can exist as construct, yet still not be a part of our world.

PLATO: You speak rightly. And you also convince me that each new thing we find opens up ever more gaps for what we cannot see. Even if other worlds of things did arise from our own finite one, we would simply have more Forms and yet more enormous but empty space, around us, among us and over us, still of identifiable number, without passing into the actual infinite. If actually infinite, and beyond our measure and sense, gentle nudges from those unknowable places could happen at any time. We would have no means to be aware of the effect and no way to gain true knowledge of its Form nor how it came to be. The earliest response was to write stories. Our own answer can only take the form of blind responses, in how we live our lives, in the choices we make for our own actions in the world. It might include stories. Much like the Love you spoke of, which seems to ever expand, the infinite can indeed be right there inside our minds! Unknowable--unreachable--untouchable. But exist? Yes, but necessarily outside of our world. The infinite can be everywhere and nowhere at the same time.

The evolution of thinking

Nature of the infinite

SARAH: Communication between that outside space and our world can only go in one direction, perhaps only to those who wish and choose to hear it. I can tell a friend that I have heard some words or have some things inside my head, but, unless he has heard them too, he cannot know of what I speak, nor can I prove or share my inspiration. The images and ideas are in my mind, so he cannot know or share them, only what I tell him. Words, written or spoken, are not the thing itself. I can shout words back towards the infinite, yet remain unable to see them arrive. I am named for one who bore a child when she was a very old woman, far beyond the years for a woman to bear children. How can I doubt such touches from outside our world?

PLATO: Surely you cannot, nor can I. Since this outside space is where the gaps between what we can know about a thing and the thing itself reside, it no longer surprises that such an abstract thing as Virtue cannot be

Justice, Beauty, etc. are special constructs

taught, only learned. And that Beauty cannot take the same shape to every being. That Justice can prove so elusive for any worldly collection of men, viewed differently by each.

SARAH: A bounty of created richness that cannot be pinned to mere things.

PLATO: All these ideas are found as much in our first intuition as in the resultant negations which lead to an endless back and forth. The once dominant disappears. Apparent unity of thought fragments into pieces, only to recombine in a new guise. My Soul is most content, now that its nature has come into clearer focus as an enabler and an assembler.

SARAH: This seems a complexity which is not complex.

The Soul and judgment

PLATO: Perhaps the Form of a Soul is found as some part of the infinite inside of me, present yet unknowable. I can see clearly that both the description and the judgment or reshaping of such a Form cannot lie in the hands of a single man or a group of men, nor can it be static. If described by one, then judgment must lie elsewhere; to say otherwise would be to claim to take the infinite and place it among the things of the world, a deceptive folly. With all this clarity, my Soul and I can truly find an easy peace in many matters.

Speculation about God

SARAH: Dear Plato, you show right opinion and wisdom again. I see a proper name for this presence in the outside and the inside spaces, a simpler name. I will not try to understand it as a thing of the world. Surely it is what is known as God.

PLATO: That seems to differ from my multiplicity of gods?

SARAH: Perhaps not really. For me, just God. Whether He or She or It, He fills the gaps, the outside and the inside of the never-to-be-known. A personal God of caring relationship, Love if you like, within me and around me, the same as yours, whether either of us knows it or cares. He must be truly infinite, in power, in knowledge, in presence, in permanence, and can thus only be one. My words to Him can only serve to open up myself to hear and see and act. Only through my own responses do I know if contact has been made. Myself and my soul are all I manage. All final judgment of my soul and my responses, to the things of the world and to my own constructs and models, fall solely into His care. No other choice makes sense. The realm of God is the home of a truly infinite 'all.' Any kingdom seen by man is simply a tiny speck inside of that infinite.

Nature of God

PLATO: Whether your name of God is the same as the one which I or anyone else might use simply does not matter. Much sense seems to come from the possibility of such a resolution, recognized or not by me. If peace has come, what more can one ask?

SARAH: It is late, and I share your peace. I wish you much success wherever your path may lead; you are indeed a gift to your students.

JOHN: And thus you parted. So tell me, friend Sarah, how did I do? Was I as complete as you would wish? Please forgive my not-so-subtle ways.

SARAH: Oh, John, you are such a rascal with your listening in. Complete? Yes. Muddled again, as conversations usually are. You do again amaze me. Having thought a bit yourself about the discussion, did you learn as much as I? It was an instructive and unexpected encounter for me.

JOHN: You know, Sarah, such meetings no longer surprise me. So much seems told to us in ways that we cannot fathom. As I think about your discussion, I am drawn into the fullness of my own experience. When I reflect on theology, most other thinkers in that field seem to share a tacit assumption of the universality of the universe, meaning that, in some sense, their 'infinite' God is also a part of the universe. That assumption must be false. No matter. All theories evolve and seek refinement.

Limitations on God

SARAH: On the other side of the coin, among scientific writers, when a God or Creator is even seriously considered, the same tacit assumption prevails. And they limit or circumscribe their discussion in other ways. First, God must somehow have a similar kind of 'existence' to that of other scientifically-observable phenomena. Or second, that only the mechanics of those phenomena are on the table, either being possible or impossible without a Creator. Or third, writers with such beliefs fall into a semantic debate about where and how He exists in the world, rather than examining assumptions which might be faulty and have limited their vision.

JOHN: I sense a passion once again. But does not all of this distract us from the reasons why you were so eager to meet with Plato himself? We can easily let speculation distract from facts and truth.

SARAH: Indeed we can. You are so good to set the spurs to me from time to time, or perhaps withdraw the spurs I set to myself.

JOHN: Let us get back to where we left off when we discussed the conversation between Euclid and Plato.

SARAH: Quite so. We charged ourselves with exploration of the possibility for the existence of a mind-to-mind gap, to add to our collection of the ematomic. That possibility became the impetus for my own discussions with Plato.

JOHN: The separateness of ourselves as individuals leads to great difficulties in any understanding of a commonalty of ideas and constructs. Even though philosophers are not biologists nor psychologists, they have identified this difficulty. It is an unbridgeable gap, to use your earlier words, mind separated from mind, both gap and trap. A wall.

Our separateness as individuals

SARAH: Yes, another instance of the universe's gaps, the last of the mind and matter gaps which make up the ematomic wall, and just as countable as the earlier ones. From my studies, I recall that C.G. Jung used the term *collective unconscious* as an explanation to bridge this final gap, probably visualizing results and consequences very similar to our own, despite a different framework and purpose. Others have suggested as well that the entire universe is mind, a thought we mentioned earlier.

JOHN: My sense is that such formalities have no consequence. Your ematomic gaps seem inescapable reality. The resultant true consequences for the nature of things flows from those gaps. If the mind-to-mind gap did not exist, only one blob of mind would be left, and where is the utility in such a description or circumstance? A proof is often considered to exist by the absurdity of its negation. What could be more absurd than a single blob for all of humanity? All becomes observer, with nothing to observe. Our premise is that observers must exist, so existence cannot be conclusion as well. Not even the existence of two *separate* observers would remain. Everything becomes a study of constructs, not reality.

I think, therefore I am

SARAH: There are other matters of science. In the question of the permanence of the things of the world, there will always be matters for further exploration. Ever smaller objects will doubtless continue to be discovered. Since destruction and creation appear to mostly happen at the very extrema of the space-time curvature, with status as matter or energy irrelevant, neither affects the finiteness of the universe, a conclusion reached by those who measure such a sum-total as well. Nor will it alter the ematomic wall made up of the three unbridgeable gaps that we have exposed. Mind-to-matter, matter-to-mind, mind-to-mind. The fourth one, matter-to-matter, can perhaps be explored by the tools we use for all exploration including what we call void or empty space. Even if creation and destruction are part of the continuum of how matter works, probability difficulties will still overwhelm for the examination of any particular existing combination or status of matter and energy.

JOHN: In this third question of our individuality, our separateness from others, combined with the earlier topics, it seems more difficult and certainly illogical for those who do not choose to explore the ematomic gaps themselves to sustain their unwillingness. Neither the serious scientist nor the philosopher ought to dodge the exploration, whether one treats with the mind or with our world. The gossamer steel curtain of the ematomic wall affects both and limits both, whether recognized or not.

SARAH: Absolutely. It assuredly cannot be proven that exploration of the ematomic gaps leads to a Creator —my God. But even the shallowest consideration does make it impossible to disprove the existence of such a Prime Mover. That consequence is likely the more significant and the harder sell.

JOHN: I sense your passions starting to heat up.

SARAH: The infinite is a tricky place. The notion of consequential creation without outside resources available is problematic, becoming more of a reshuffling than a true creation. Any "start" is always problematic. It is much easier if one simply supposes the presence of the needed supply of such resources, a premise. Our own premise has been simply that objects and motion exist, not how they came to be. For the infinite itself, the question has no meaning. The essence of our world and the infinite might or might not be changed by the existence of both, but we could not prove the matter either way.

How do "starts" happen?

JOHN: I agree that additional objects, or fewer, would not change the essence.

SARAH: Some seem to find the world intolerable with us humans being what we are. Even as they criticize, they direct their gaze outward rather than inward, seldom including themselves within its scope. Better to hold up a mirror. For myself, I find it more intolerable to imagine a world with the absence of our human-ness. Our frailties most especially. For each of us, our own warts may be removable; our being is not.

JOHN: Well said. Thoughtful examination may give us a precise scalpel for our warts, but it remains to each of us to use such a tool with wisdom and discernment. Surely such a gift, whatever its source, must be a part of our being human.

SARAH: I'll shift to another argument which has been put forward, a look at randomness versus order. Can random processes, whether outside or inside our world, either create or maintain the precise orderliness of our world, including all of its proven processes. Can they lead to all of the motivations, feelings and wishes of humankind? Possibly possible, but I must seriously doubt it.

JOHN: I had always understood that the natural consequence of motion is towards greater disorder, not less.

Orderliness is improbable

SARAH: Those implications are best left to others, and do not seem to me to matter. Taking a finite, but unordered, universe and evolving it into the highly organized one we see about us, in the time frame we know to exist, makes a mockery of probability. Yes, I know that there remains extraordinary chaos today. The existence of motion does make anything possible, but as it does so, it also obliterates probability calculations. Careful students of probabilistic implications and realities, such as F.S. Collins in *The Language of God* and A.D. Aczel in *Why Science Does Not Disprove God*, have shown a great deal of well-reasoned skepticism. As a scientist, Aczel goes much further, showing proofs beyond our capabilities, but speculations of a somewhat similar nature.

JOHN: We are here today. How is it that such a degree of order is present around us precisely today? Orderliness abounds and an orderliness into which we fit and seem to have always fit. It is understandable that we cannot achieve orderliness in such things as Justice and Goodness and Beauty, or even mathematics, due to the limited means of transfer between myriad human minds as you and Plato discussed. But how does one then easily suppose the achievement of orderliness in everything else? In mathematics, randomness has consequences, one of them being the unlikeliness of order.

The anthropic principle

SARAH: Aczel and others identify the presence of the present as the "anthropic principle." He shows why it is a scientific and mathematical dead-end. If one suspends a requirement for *necessity* as a part of proof, accepting the teleological construct that purpose may be part of cause itself, naturally the dead-end disappears. But other problems surface.

JOHN: All of that is just construct, with no method of proof within the realm of science, so you are taking us afield. We have tacitly agreed on two premises, with one of them being the existence of objects in motion. If you add the anthropic layer of purpose, you are taking me into constructs that seem to distract rather than clarify. Constructs arise separately out of our second premise which requires an observer or two who can create them. The ematomic wall makes it impossible to combine those two premises in the manner these arguments require.

SARAH: There are other difficulties which only depend very indirectly on the ematomic.

JOHN: You will have to clarify for me.

SARAH: There are a multiplicity of unresolved matters in science, of which three are so enigmatic that there is currently no semblance of a viable scientific theory for even one, nor even a conception of what potential experimentation might look like. First, the Big Bang theory seems to have merit. But it does not even pretend to answer the question of how matter, energy and the laws that govern them, emerged in the first place. Second, given the Big Bang, how did those assuredly dead items combine into life which emerged a great deal later under any time scale? Life has its own Darwinian processes—the complexity difference between the matter created during a Big Bang and living material is astonishing. Third, given the Big Bang, with life coming later, how did unique human-ness arise out of that mix, another astonishing complexity, with language, concepts of morality and an appreciation of beauty? Science has not come close to proposing potential replication nor experimentation. Not even theories which might suggest how such an appearance might happen. Nor has philosophy had any more success in analyzing the physical realm for these changes.

Unresolved matters in science

Matter, life, humans

JOHN: You are better at the science than I, but I feel that you choose these three questions because they may lead us in yet another direction.

SARAH: You read my mind, but I am happy to postpone the discussion for another day. From what we have learned, I would sum up the matter in this way.

Speculations lead to more speculations

Dealing honestly with infinity and the infinitely large inescapably requires faith because those matters are outside of our world. The faith of science is that the ematomic wall, the mind-to-matter and mind-to-mind gaps, has no use nor meaning nor import and can be ignored. That each part of the ematomic exists cannot be denied. They are reality as we have shown. It seems ironic that a serious scientist can talk knowingly about a butterfly effect, using constructs such as chaos or information theory, might deny that the ematomic gaps have import. Such proponents also operate as if there is no mind-to-mind gap, and that some current construct for space and time, or space-time, is a universal image of reality, making it in fact become their reality. Such denial has never worked in the past, but experience is considered irrelevant. Even as varying concepts of infinity are used, neither those variable meanings nor their implications are considered.

Faith

JOHN: In an eagerness to avoid the use of the word "faith," they employ it unawares! You were right to suggest that unanswered basics and unstated premises can lead to questionable results, a matter for another day. Without identifying their premises, they can casually use constructs to somehow conflate every aspect of human-ness with other objects as though both comprise an easy totality, subject to the same rules and manner of analysis.

SARAH: In fairness, philosophers have readily fallen into the same trap. But scientific theories change radically over time, as do philosophical ones. Both seem quicksand for *any* type of faith, let alone a precarious one. Neither requires that necessity be demonstrated. Both avoid identified premises.

JOHN: It seems unwise to label such a precarious faith as an 'examined' one.

SARAH: As one contemplates the ematomic and its role, it seems useful to consider two possible approaches. One is to get just as close to both the knowable and the unknowable as we can, removing ematomic layers. Put another way, cannot we better understand the real world by getting as close as we can to all of its objects and motions and other beings? Or are we better served by construct, with the false intimacy of description which has been created without identifiable gaps? We can avoid substance and reality entirely, except when our baby cries or we are forced into line to get groceries. From a TV screen, we get only constructs. We can avoid the beating hearts of our neighbors.

Minimizing the ematomic or layering it?

JOHN: The answer seems obvious.

SARAH: The legal profession has answered the question by allowing only direct testimony in court. But the current thrust of education, exploration and commentary is to interpose ever more gaps between ourselves and the things of the world, confusing an exponential explosion of knowledge with one of wisdom, pretending that belief and knowledge are the same. Losing touch with the real is another way to put it. Each translator and intermediary, if human, adds one ematomic layer, construct instead of the real. If electronic, the number of layers is unknown, and direct connection is replaced by an illusion of connection and intimacy. The growth and education of our young is truly important, but the biological part of human growth is known. Our senses, plus perception of objects, motion and other humans are its building blocks. The blocks are changed in crucial ways when constructs, which multiply so

Impact of the ematomic on lives

readily, replace reality. There is limited capacity in our lives, in our brains, in our moments.

JOHN: I hear a plea for reflective thought about our increasingly indirect contacts and sources. Fact versus fiction becomes a jumble.

SARAH: Actually, a plea for wisdom in every guise. An eminent scientist, S.J. Gould, made a plea for consistent use of what he called *"non-overlapping magisteria."* As construct, such a separation into areas which have differing rules for discourse and differing requirements for quality control, has compelling logic. As science, it sadly by-passes the obvious reality that we are both the observer and the observed. The *magisteria* factually *do* overlap, a reality that no construct can change.

JOHN: That seems another consequence of a failure to recognize the ematomic.

SARAH: Focus on some more distant constructs rather than the elusive objects they represent gives us an easy peace. We like to be able to create our own rules. But the ematomic identifies the uncertainty principle for humans and constructs just as Heisenberg identified one for objects.

JOHN: Examples would help me.

Examples of ematomic layers

SARAH: Consider two simple matters, the food we put into our body and the drops of rain that hit us. Today we have an enormously complicated network of constructs to let me know weeks in advance how many raindrops are hitting me as we speak. Despite those constructs which have become all that I know of the matter, I am certainly being hit by the drops that I am hit by, objects in motion. Readily observable, with no ematomic layer.

JOHN: I would say that you jest, but I know better.

SARAH: Almost every bite of food that I put in my mouth by my own choice sits at the end of an extraordinarily complex web of constructs to advise me about that bite, ematomic layers. Seldom do I just pick an apple off a tree that I have seen from birth. Every portion of each network of constructs has its own created rules for quality control; the apple is what I put in my mouth, to kill or to nourish.

JOHN: What I hear you saying is that once some object becomes immersed in the coloration of the constructs, and the language and the processes with which everyone surrounds it, the object itself can almost seem irrelevant, impossible and unnecessary. Unknowable ematomic effects hide the reality.

SARAH: Those blinders increasingly burden us. Every part of the process, including the result, is construct, despite the intervening objects. The whole activity relates more to my human-ness than to my alive-ness, but still separates me from consciousness of the object itself. It matters little whether the resulting perception is conscious or unconscious, direct observation or dream. The reality is that the number of constructs available to me has come to increasingly overwhelm the number of actual sensory perceptions that remain in my brain.

JOHN: I could not agree more. The capacity of our brains is limited, and probably fixed after our early growth is complete. If filled to overflowing with constructs, it becomes harder for perceptions to crowd them out. Quality control comes to depend on others more interested in sales than truth.

SARAH: The resolution for me lies in three separate faiths. First, I must acknowledge the existence and the value of the infinite, however unknowable, not just as a construct but as a reality, albeit clearly outside of our universe and direct experience, accepting as well that we

Three faiths

can never adequately approach "things." If that is premise, so be it, another word for faith perhaps. Second, I must exploit the role and value of science to learn the how and the ways of the finite, using models and abstractions as useful surrogates for "things" themselves and accepting that our ability to understand is limited by the ematomic gaps we cannot bridge. With models and abstractions, our proofs are constrained only by the agreements we reach about the nature of proof, our method of quality control. And third, I must posit timely nudges between the two, also unknowable, that expressly make us human and make the world whole. I feel that this approach to faith gives a more honest and robust picture, as well as one with sounder grounding in demonstrable realities. It gives both sufficiency and necessity.

JOHN: Necessities call me in other directions. You have now used the word "faith" as opposed to "premise" on several occasions, just as you did with Plato. There is more to explore.

SARAH: Indeed, so let us meet tomorrow. Sad that there is no time for a glass of wine.

Divergent Paths

JOHN: How is it, dear Sarah, that you are able to appear so refreshed and ready to go once again?

SARAH: That is amusing because I would have said exactly the same of you, dearer John. You do exhaust and amaze me.

JOHN: When you discussed the matter of our minds with Plato, you raised things which we have not yet discussed. You used the word "God" as well, which seems rather restrictive.

SARAH: We have spent much time on the factual and provable things about our world, as we explored first with Plato, Solomon and Euclid. But just as the scientist S.A. Hawking did at the end of his last book, let us also speculate, for instruction as well as fun. The identified ematomic can be a launching pad, not only unrecognized dilemmas which have led every philosopher into a variety of subterfuge. Perhaps philosophy can be more than therapy for the mind, as thoughtfully proposed recently. The unknowable must be recognized as such. We need not fear divergent paths, but embrace and enjoy them.

Fact vs speculation

JOHN: Diverge away. Let's seek both joy and learning.

SARAH: There is much still to consider. However, the very first fact from the ematomic wall is that our individual paths necessarily diverge, from moment to moment, from day to day, from person to person. A matter to celebrate, even though we can only choose one path, our own. Another Huxley observation.

JOHN: I stand with my head down for having forgotten!

SARAH: As do too many of your fellow humans, probably with the poet Frost excepted. Good poets never

The ematomic limits us

have their heads down and give us exits. Let us go back to the arguments against the existence of an outside presence such as God. That argument is often stated using purported principles of science, trying to discover facts about what must be infinite from the finite world of reality. We have shown quite conclusively that the existence of the ematomic, when combined with the finite reality of the world, makes proof of either the existence or non-existence of a meaningful God impossible. Arguments against the existence of God cannot lead to verifiable truth. Whatever cannot be verified, a prerequisite for the scientist, falls into the realm of premise, or belief, as contrasted with knowledge.

JOHN: There *is* underlying truth to the matter of the existence of an infinite presence, whether or not we are able to know anything about it. Facts are facts, whether or not we know them. Let us go back to those who deny an infinite presence.

SARAH: Those who rely on science tend to pick *ad hoc* time and probability scales, varying their measures to suit the goals of each argument. Some end up by making both God and where He resides far too small. Some inaccurately apply the calculus of the truly large or small. Some impose a concept of 'time' on matters which are only poorly perceived through the existence of motion. All use constructs without hesitation, even though those are only a personal reality, untransferable to others. None explain an infinite God within a finite universe, yet use such a God for their argument, promoting the distraction that such might be possible.

JOHN: Are you saying that they become a bit self-centered in focusing on their own constructs and the arguments they use?

SARAH: You state the matter well. We must become self-centered: our constructs are our own, whether of the received or of the created type. But we do not need to become self-absorbed. Science is a glorious realm of its own, but scientists frustrate rational discussion by granting the freedom of evolution to the writings and theories of science while withholding the same freedom from other disciplines. They profess to seek change and refinement. But they withhold the courtesy of embracing change and refinement for other types of thinkers, dismissing evolution which might occur in other fields. Consider the silliness that was once put forward as "God being in the gaps." How could one even conceive of such a tiny God, supposed to exist solely in the physical gaps between the objects of the world? Furthermore, those spatial gaps shrink as scientific knowledge expands. They are an insignificant portion of an ematomic entirety. Such a God could not bear any resemblance to the infinitely expansive God that I discussed with Plato. To describe those alternative constructions merely as 'limited' seems generous. Even for speculation, let us try to keep our own feet firmly on solid ground.

Being even-handed

JOHN: Quite so. And I seem to have stirred up a matter of passion for you. Tut, tut. Generosity must extend to all. In their defense, what we observe necessarily resides completely inside our universe, so it is natural for vision to be constricted. Our natural world gives a richness of observable processes which overwhelms. It is hard to conceive any limits.

SARAH: Also in their defense, the proofs of mathematics, which often rely on the concept of infinity, are not available to physical science. It can only draw probabilistic conclusions from actual observations. Life sciences also have great bounty. But neither has the exhaustive supply of samples or examples needed for proof that one factual observation is both a *necessary* and a *sufficient* cause for another fact. Results from the world around us only have probabilistic truth, not absolute or fully verifiable truth such as you and I seek. In other words, scientists are restricted to showing *sufficiency*. To

Limits on tools available

establish necessity, they must use models or constructs. Or they can move to shaky ground by adding purpose to natural process, trying to withhold the element of intent as they do so. If *intent* is added to their process, then an *intender* must follow.

JOHN: It is easy for our minds and outlooks to become confused by the tools we choose to use, taking leaps back and forth from the world of our constructs into the real world of objects. We do so without reflecting on the jump we have just made over the ematomic wall which separates mind from matter, and which separates our two minds. How easy it is to come to believe that more cannot possibly be needed.

Separated minds = separated environments

SARAH: Not to mention that our separated two must also necessarily each have its own separated environs. To go on, there are forces which repel, creating objects; and forces which attract, causing motion. Those are the forces of an observable world. That world also requires an observer, and a listener in order to demonstrate truths! The observed world is what we seek to understand, with only what we can perceive actually available to our minds to lead us to understanding.

JOHN: Such has been one central focus for philosophers throughout the ages, but, as thinkers, they must work within their own separated world of constructs to put together pieces of understanding. Conversation gives the illusion of commonalty.

SARAH: The presence of the ematomic gap of mind-to-matter has led to ever more elaborate theories for how one might bridge the gap. In his book, *Mind and Cosmos: Why the Materialist Neo-Darwinian Conception of Nature Is Almost Certainly False*, the philosopher T. Nagel considers the matter in detail. He identifies a part of the problem for which the reductive materialism of modern science ought to, but does not, have any viable theory, namely that the constructs of our minds have an objective reality which is different from that of other perceived objects of the world. He suggests other constructs as alternatives for bridging the gap.

JOHN: That different approach is an appropriate subject for inquiry about the world. It is distinct from our premises which require only that both an observer and an observed exist. A premise is unprovable description, leaving alternatives for others who may not accept the premise, even if they do not state their own. Often the need for an observer is the element which gets omitted.

SARAH: It is tempting to take the fact that something *can* happen via observable processes to thereby turn the fact of its occurrence into a necessary proof of entire causality, that is, that it *must* have happened thus. However, "if A, then B" is not the same as "if B, then A." Causality cannot be proven in reverse.

Establishing causality

JOHN: There is alternative potential truth when cause is involved. B may not be able to be caused unless its existence requires that there be something intrinsic to A which only allows A to serve as the cause. Such is called *purposeful* (or end-driven) causality, a teleological logic, if you will forgive the redundancy of wording.

SARAH: That approach translates to "if, and only if, A, then B;" but an exhaustive search is required for proof, an alternative not available to science. At best, we can only describe an isolated and bounded portion of the processes in play. Those processes always exist in conjunction with many other processes, whether in the organism, the community or our entire world. Accurate use of probabilities in analyzing such a multitude of processes is also rare, too much a specialist's realm.

JOHN: I have heard the terms "natural selection," "intelligent design" and "teleological process." All seem to lead to quite a stir of controversy about the "how" of our world.

Intelligent design

SARAH: Quite so. You seem to be trying to diffuse my passion. Some persons consider one or the other alternative to be a complete and mutually-exclusive description of the processes of our world.

The necessity of an agent

JOHN: A teleological process arises when the purpose or end result of the process is a necessary cause for the starting point itself. It might seem a third alternative to the first two. However, any notion of purpose without an identified agent makes no sense. If the agent is identified, the process does not differ from intelligent design. If not, the reasoning is circular: the result alone requires the cause which in turn requires the result. Without an agent, the process is merely sufficient, not necessary, because there can be many other sufficient processes. Yet there is passion for each alternative.

"Value:" independent of survival alone

SARAH: Purpose also suggests value, that certain things are intrinsically better than others. If that value only relates to survival, then the argument has gone in a circle: x is better than y solely because x survives, but its survival is what defines x as being better. Since all are constructs, they can be as we wish them, a problem for demonstrated truth, and for much of this line of related reasoning.

JOHN: In other words, we are free to label as magic or delusion what we wish! Or pick another choice: the unknown.

The factually finite world restricts choice

SARAH: I mentioned earlier the thinker C.S. Lewis. With his consummate writing and thinking skills, if he had lived to see a proof that the universe is finite, he might likely have stated most of our conclusions far more thoroughly and eloquently. I think he would have suggested that examined faith gives us the wonderful gift of another precise scalpel to help us remove these warts, rather than trying to do it on our own. It remains to each of us to use such a tool with wisdom and discernment.

JOHN: Your reference must be to what we think of today as religion. Is that a concise or a broad conclusion?

SARAH: Before I address your question more specifically, let me say that there are many ways one could put together religious approaches, as distinct from religion itself, to arrive at a satisfactory combination. People have done so throughout the centuries, facing their struggle to figure out how to deal with a puzzling part of their biologic nature, an apparent spiritual component. The harder problem comes for the many who deny one essential building block, that of faith itself. And let me use the word 'faith' instead of 'premise.' The two are not quite the same thing. Religionists generally make faith a routine component, even as they may limit and deny many other necessary building blocks. Faith is not as specific nor as directed as premise, nor does it require even definitional clarity. It seems mystery.

Faith as an alternative

JOHN: I agree with the distinction. Our language can be so imprecise.

SARAH: Regardless of the pathway for study, it is one thing to note the world as it is and quite another to model or to visualize it a way which seems a convenient fit for a useful portion of what is. Any construct can appear to obey whatever laws or restrictions we place upon it. Religion can be a construct, but I would prefer not to restrict its possibilities in such a way.

Premises require precise thinking

JOHN: You understand the intent of my question. Our conversations have made some form of faith inescapable, but with impenetrabilities that we ought to consider. There are things which are demonstrably unknowable. Oh, does that grate on our sensibilities and our training, and our egos! Instead it should prompt us to explore the deeper reasons. Back to the matter of religion: does it give us guidance for the ematomic?

Ematomic: objects vs constructs

A conscious Spirit

SARAH: My learning and experience in this area is pretty much limited to the Bible, but a study of multiple religions, the historic home for the idea of faith and morality, may well give guidance. To visit our friend Hegel and to use his wording, I would put it this way. The Spirit of the Old Testament has *consciousness*. Under such guidance, we do the 'right' thing, if indeed we do, because of an urging Spirit that wishes that it to be so. The meaning of 'right' is a matter from Spirit, demanding obedience to Its commands and definitions. Spirit gave us ten commands, plus hundreds of additional rules, which have nudged us in the direction of doing the 'right' thing. From the earliest records, such things as laws were the first constructs to emerge in written form, with considerations about Spirit closely behind.

JOHN: You give a different description, but the concepts are much as I have heard.

A self-conscious Spirit

SARAH: Then the whole framework was changed by what was called a New Covenant. The transformed Spirit of the New Testament is *self-conscious* as well, possessing full understanding that Spirit, in and of Itself, is intimately present in our human choices and their results, whether we either seek or accept that presence or not. Under that form of guidance, we do the 'right' thing, if indeed we do, because, as humans, we *need to*, because we have discovered that Spirit and Its presence have become a part of ourselves. It has led us unknowingly into an imperative to act in such a way, at least in that instance. We do not act solely because of a specific command, some 'law.' The nudge has become even more internal than external. The actual nature of Spirit is not as important as our *belief* in It.

JOHN: Again, I have heard similar thoughts, but I like your alternative descriptions.

SARAH: The fact that humans care about other humans, even remote humans, suggests to me that self-conscious Spirit is at work in us and is part of our human-ness. We have an urge to do the 'right thing.'

JOHN: That seems a good speculation.

SARAH: Christians have sustained for far too long notions from the Old Testament, such as the possibility of heresy and other forms of factual domination by humans and their decisions, even over the very domain of God. We are imperfect in how we accept and understand Spirit, but have often followed a pathway which tries to put ourselves in charge. Doubtless other religions have found their own relationship with Spirit, but such is my view of Christianity with its troubled past and, sadly, present.

Human meddling

JOHN: Concise, if conciseness can also be lengthy.

SARAH: You appreciate clarity as well, so let me give you examples, in fact going back to my sample of three enigmatic puzzles for science. Your memory needs no refreshing, but mine does, so here they are. First, there was the creation of something out of nothing, leading to the Big Bang. Second, the creation of life and living material out of dead material. Third, the creation of consciousness and human-ness out of simple living material.

Three enigmas for science

JOHN: I think I can see where you are headed. You told me that science has no viable theory to account for any of the three.

SARAH: None that I have found. The fascinating thing is that while science still has no useful theory for any of the three, the Bible gives a quite specific answer for each, in materials which are more than two thousand years old. The creation out of nothing was a specific nudge from an infinite God;   as infinite, His dwelling and duration is beyond the scope of anything knowable. But He is all-

Answers from the Bible

powerful, with everything within His capabilities for all time, including a creation from nothing. All of our human time is compressed within a single finger-snap for anything infinite, so how time is described is immaterial. The second answer is another specific nudge from God, creating life and animals from rocks and thin air, alive but not necessarily human as we would define the distinction. The third was yet another nudge from God, putting the Word (Himself who has existed for all time) into action, creating human-ness into a portion of the alive-ness which was created by the earlier nudge.

JOHN: Clearly stated. If able, I might have said the same myself.

Can animals sin?

SARAH: It is interesting as well that our ability to *sin* seems coincident with our ability to create constructs, our human-ness. Sin is defined by excess. Animals and plants do not sin. At least that is what I observe, even given our limited range of words to choose. And we must make the choices at times without definitive evidence.

JOHN: I agree with those thoughts as well.

A fourth nudge

SARAH: To go on, there is a fourth identifiable nudge in the form of the New Covenant which changed the morality of "an eye for an eye" into one of loving every neighbor in a total way, leaving the matters of God to God alone. It is hard for me to fault the plausibility of any of these four nudges as explanatory, albeit not demonstrable, reality. All preceded by many centuries any vision by scientists which might propose alternative theories, even for the first three. The fourth also answers the morality portion of human-ness which was identified by the respected teacher S.J. Gould as a '*magisterium* inaccessible to science.'

JOHN: Even though you think as a scientist, you continue to surprise me with philosophy.

SARAH: Another interesting matter is the detail of the history. The earliest recorded conceptions of Spirit, in the Old Testament and other places, are clear that It is inscrutable, cannot be observed and that it is very risky to try to do so, even resulting in death, the end of both aliveness and human-ness.

JOHN: There is much repetition of those fears in the Bible, especially the Old Testament.

SARAH: The characteristics of Spirit as a law-giver, along with possessing power, omnipresence, and permanence, exist from the earliest formulations. They coincide with the biological emergence of our human ability to create constructs. Knowledge also occupies a special place in the earliest stories, at first being a simple need by Spirit for humans to understand laws and morality. Later Spirit saw that a *conversation* with humans was needed as well, in order that Its commands and desires be faithfully and consistently carried out.

History of constructs

JOHN: As I recall, those early recordings are only several thousand years old.

SARAH: It is interesting as well that you mention the timing. Since the constructs of our minds, or that which makes us human, immediately spawn new constructs, likely multiplying exponentially much as cells divide, one could use calculations based on the timing of those early records to determine when our first human-ness might have appeared. Prior to our first constructs, we would have only been alive, without human-ness. Before those first recorded constructs, the earlier records are pictorial, being purely of objects or observed events. They do not necessarily reflect human-ness, only alive-ness. Once a being could process perceptions into constructs, a transformative explosion began, a different matter indeed from our first simple alive-ness.

Exponential growth

JOHN: Matters for further exploration are always before us. Such a reverse calculation seems simple.

SARAH: And here we are. To go further, the idea that any particular person was the 'first' to have a particular construct seems unknowable. Whether something is discovery, or merely a new formulation, is elusive. Only a tiny fraction of constructs get recorded, and most recording techniques are not as perfect as we would like to suppose. We cannot escape the ematomic mind-matter gaps of words.

JOHN: Our egos can get in our way;   constructs can blind us.

The new-born baby

SARAH: These matters might be similar for a baby starting at its creation.   First, as simple cells, a new person may only have alive-ness.   Human-ness comes when the ability to perceive motion and objects gradually becomes an ability to merge those perceptions into constructs.   To amplify the matter another way, only the ability to perceive via sensory receptors, plus the brain structure itself, can be transmitted via DNA to successive generations.   It is part of the conceived baby.   But the DNA cannot transmit *what* we perceive, the *content*, whether simple observations or the succeeding layers of constructs, only methods of perceiving and thinking.   The explosion of constructs, as well as all other perceptions, must start afresh for each newborn baby.   Both alive-ness and human-ness are present, the alive-ness containing eons of developed capabilities, but the other empty.   The human-ness   starts anew in each newborn in its first combination of perceptions into construct.

JOHN: Interesting thoughts!

Divergence of process

SARAH: Constructs in each new-born demonstrate change itself, and only survive thanks to an ematomic process.   DNA survives through a physical process, observable because the construct we have labelled persistence assists us. Quality control for the DNA versus that of the independent constructs is on differing time-scales and happens in different ways. The death and mutation of constructs is hidden from the view of any separated two of us, but the similarities suggest a connection even if we cannot prove it. For ourselves, we have both human-ness and alive-ness. As unique beings, with one life, each of us must face and manage the realities of our own environment on our own.

JOHN: When we promote conformity, we seem determined to destroy that which gives us a reason to exist. Conformity and empathy are not the same.

SARAH: For the entirety of humans, moving away from a single newborn, a recent book by S.J. Greenblatt, titled *The Rise and Fall of Adam and Eve*, although focused on human constructs, gives linguistic evidence for the relationship with Spirit in its first law-giving guise, plus support for our evolutionary time-line. His *Early Spirit* examples of a separated emergence for human-ness are compelling. Instead of relying on interpreters, he might better have studied the words of one with your same name who wrote a succinct version of the Adam and Eve story. Greenblatt quotes it: "In the beginning was the Word, and the Word was with God, and the Word was God." Elegant writing. It answers all of science's unanswerables as it weaves together Old Testament theology, focused on place via the permanence of stones which God can make live and speak, with transformation into the New Testament theology of direct human relationship with God. All four of our earlier questions are answered in a single sentence, succinctly describing the nudges. The sentence is construct. It is speculation, not proof, but evidence nonetheless. Constructs identify our human-ness, often, even always, being our only tools.

JOHN: How is it that you are never content with a single aspect of your story?

The ematomic and overlapping magisteria

SARAH: In further irony, as the final six words of his book *Rocks of Ages* where he discusses *magisteria*, S.J. Gould quotes exactly the same words as Greenblatt, albeit just the first of its three phrases. His plea for an easy peace among all *magisteria* is better addressed by achieving greater clarity over the role of the ematomic as we have discovered. The two missing phrases, if from an existent God, highlight once again why the *magisteria* do indeed, and must necessarily, overlap.

JOHN: The failure to identify the ematomic has forced thinkers into alternatives which close rather than open doors, both in science and in philosophy. I cannot speak authoritatively on science. You might rudely point out that, since all of our words are our own construct, we cannot speak authoritatively on anything. The ematomic precludes it. However, by speaking together, we can put matters out there for others to consider and use. Conversations.

Quality control for constructs

SARAH: To get back to the early history, although I did not intend to digress even this far, a perceived later need by humans for an expanded and more effective relationship with Spirit coincides with the addition of self-consciousness, at least insofar as the Old Testament passed to the New. As an adaptation loop for an effective quality control over constructs, a conversational and participatory Spirit seems far better suited to help us deal with the matter-to-mind and mind-to-mind gaps. It is also better adapted to our human-ness.

JOHN: It remains true enough that these choices must have their basis in faith. Even so, the extent and nature of what you suggest is illuminating. If I close my eyes, and mind, I can feel that I have jumped the ematomic wall between myself and every other being, and between every name and every object.

SARAH: These examples show a faith far removed from what we have been discussing, but consequential in its own right. While the existence of God or Spirit is not provable, even if Hegel might have thought otherwise, my own faith gets great comfort from myriad things which I see as support for the notion of gentle nudges from such a source. Let me give a few examples, directed to that end.

JOHN: You divine the needs of my simple mind.

SARAH: First, I see a steady trajectory throughout history of declining human violence toward our fellow man. Even more, I see a steady increase in the nature and degree of abhorrence for such violence as does occur. Second, I see the readiness of humans to jump in with help and support of every conceivable kind whenever disasters occur, and otherwise. Morality seems hard to explain as other than a nudge since Christians are such a small minority, unlikely to impact evolution themselves. Philanthropy and charity abound. Our dependence on constructs may actually lead to greater comfort for the soul through indirect giving. Third, I notice the feelings of people in community, clearly more than a simple instinct for survival since they differ markedly from other animates. It might be shared grief at a funeral or the pleasure of doing something nice for a neighbor. Fourth, I see a steady trajectory towards a human expectation of legitimate participation in all matters governing their lives. Finally, as we said before, I see the crucial importance to people everywhere of a spiritual component in their lives, also a dominant feature of human interactions, for good and ill. Some express it by denying that they are expressing it! What irony! Even if it is never expressed exactly as I would describe my own spirituality, it still seems present in nearly every human.

Evidence of continuing nudges

JOHN: I see as well that one cannot consider such as definitive. Proof by actions and results is not possible since cause is so elusive to identify. But these matters inform. Conversations.

Narrow thinking

SARAH: Scientists such as S.A. Pinker have explored some of these trends and chosen to explain them solely in terms of a trajectory of human minds and constructs. They reject any component of spirituality. But their trajectory and model imposes purpose and value on a purely Darwinian or on any other naturalistic model. As we showed before, both value and purpose require an agent. Intentionality cannot be casually bypassed. Darwin didn't even try.

JOHN: It seems narrow-minded to assign the requisite intent to one theory of how or why things have happened without considering what seems a simpler alternative, that of Spirit. All of these matters are constructs of our own choosing. As we choose, we must not forget that there *is* underlying truth and reality to the matter, however unknowable and not of our world. As A.L. Huxley said, facts remain facts, even if unknown to us.

Commands and the ematomic

SARAH: In the New Testament, God gave two commands. The first encompasses our relationship to Spirit. The second, to love one another and ourselves, encompasses a preferred relationship to each other as humans. The second command allows us, if we choose, to transcend the ematomic gap between ourselves as humans. We are unique, and cannot possibly agree precisely with any other human about anything. We are inescapably on divergent paths, but we can still love one another.

JOHN: I see your point.

SARAH: The first command could be otherwise stated as a command to honor the entirety of the ematomic wall above all else, it being a portion of the likely residence of God. In the Old Testament, a firm command was in place for people not to explore that wall on pain of instant death.

JOHN: Surely you know of other religious perspectives?

SARAH: I have not found equally concise and useful wisdom elsewhere. But I can see how different religions, throughout the world and for all time, have used components of this same thinking, both constructively and destructively. If the concept of heresy, that there is one right way to think and act, is present, problems arise. The focus shifts away from the spiritual or moral notion of 'good' to the human and legal construct of 'right.' In other instances, if one of the two New Testament commands is missing, the result is too passive to deal with the real world. In any case, the reality of God, if He exists, is the determinant, not our conceptions and constructs.

Other religious approaches

JOHN: You seem to raise another question. Does this Spirit have need of words?

SARAH: Your question contains its own answer. Being infinite in all respects, Spirit has no need for any of our tools. It might choose to touch us by using our ever-present feelings, before those become corrupted by our human ability, first to suppress, and second, to transform and expand feelings into desires, passions and other constructs. The words we use are our own creation, one part of our attempt to try to batter our way through the gossamer steel of the impenetrable ematomic wall.

Spirit and words

JOHN: Our friends Plato, Solomon and Euclid would agree.

SARAH: Spirit has no need of words, but may well have found them useful on occasion as an extra means of communicating with us. Our own actions in response are probably a true and honest mirror of our deepest faith or

Faith into action

faiths, our inner being translated into an outer substantial self, however poorly. Since Spirit, if it exists, must reside everywhere, inside and outside of our world and ourselves, our communication will reach it regardless. But as I see it, only goodness and kindness and love give our human world of relationships glue rather than explosives. Universally applicable in all situations, just as Spirit directed. I believe it was Gandhi who suggested that we be the world we want to see. Through such actions, religion, morality, rationality, science and human-ness can make an easy peace, accepting boundaries between what we can and cannot know.

Demonstrable vs speculative truth

JOHN: In order to properly take advantage of certain truths, it seems prudent to first understand and accept them. It is a bit arrogant and wrong-headed to set ourselves above demonstrated truth. But we are humans and even though our flashlight only points in one direction, hold it we must; it shows us the cave of Plato in another guise. The ematomic are not the simple gaps of Plato, causing shadows which can be studied; its shadows are just as elusive but hold more substance. They lead us to two conclusions. First, what we have been discussing here today (except for our factual observations) has only speculative truth. But second, the ematomic wall itself is demonstrable truth.

SARAH: How strange it is that our limits and limitations have power, along with our abilities. Even questions which cannot be answered have value. It seems wiser to embrace the reality of ematomic gaps and the resultant divergences than to play the ostrich.

JOHN: An audience can decide. It is certainty that we are all on divergent paths every moment of every day. Divergent from every person we meet, whether or not we can hang out with them or get to know them. The ematomic forces us to be divergent. Even more, with each of us being unique, our environs or what surrounds is necessarily unique, and therefor divergent as well

SARAH: We can see divergence as barrier or as blessing, as problem or as opportunity. Our own biological skins cause us to be fearful of all but what we think we know and can trust most closely. Survival. We want everyone to be just like us, so that our trust and safety can feel much larger than rational thought can support.

JOHN: Just imagine what a barren place the world would be if that were actually so. You and I, who are friends, could not have had any semblance of useful discussion if our pathways were not divergent. Conversation, even thought, would be pointless. The ematomic separating us creates our uniqueness, even as it also separates us, and from every object of the world. Conversations and good choices have more value and utility than any attempt to create uniform surroundings for everyone, an impossibility.

Sources of our value

SARAH: My own strength and comfort comes from sensing a Spirit that lies in the ematomic which is with me every moment of every day. And from knowing that It is always there, whether I feel weak or afraid or ebullient or sad. It is just as self-conscious as I am and wishes to talk with me at every moment, even as I seem to wish to talk with It; even as I curse using Its name. The commands to me are to honor the ematomic and to love every single other. They are commands to do both at every moment of every day, regardless of where our divergent paths have taken us, and may take us today. It gives me an easy peace.

JOHN: What about those who say that what you call Spirit does not exist?

SARAH: It makes no difference. We are all divergent in every possible way regardless. But I *believe,* even know, and that is all I can manage. All I have to work with is myself, but having a good role-model, with the sense of a steadying hand, is helpful. That I am forgiven lifts a heavy burden from my biological and psychological self, letting me focus on the command to love every other being, known and unknown. What about you?

JOHN: I have tried to keep my own views on Spirit apart from our discussions, although I am sure you have noted references. I shall devote time to my particular skill which is to record the deeds and words of others.

SARAH: That would be an incomparable gift for us all.

JOHN: So perhaps we may meet again?

An end to the basics

SARAH: Unlikely. Once our classes finish, my portion of the search is over. You and I have uncovered more than I could have hoped. When the ematomic is combined with the world of things which we can perceive and readily explore, plus Spirit which we cannot, the status of basic questions is as clear as I could have wished. I am neither craftsman nor poet, so it is for the skilled in those pursuits to do the hard work of probing the details. Those are what matter to our lives. If we can give them extra tools, perhaps including some of what we have discussed, that would be enough. I would not be good at anything needing craft or art.

JOHN: You do most things well. Another glass of wine in joint celebration?

SARAH: An early toast then. Peace be with you.

With extra inspiration from:

Dr. Paul Young
Hailey Helm Wiseman
Doug Goodwin
John Patton
Joan Dixon
Carol Burnes
Aaron Trembath
George Chiga
Rob Daniel

*plus all those countable others who are able to keep their eyes
steadily on the truly important.*

POSTLUDE

A Prere

Love in Jesus
Jesus has love
It never runs out
Nothing is better
Than love from Jesus
Jesus saved us from Sin
So let us worship Him forever
And praise the Lord and Love him forever
Because God has the right time to take us to heaven
So sing to the Lord, and he loves us dearly.
Let us see your face when we go there.

In God's name
Amen

Sarah, 6, at a memorial service for her great-grandmother Sarah, 91
April 2011
(used by permission)

Bibliography & Further Reading

Abbott, E.A., *Flatland, 1884*

Aczel, A.D., *various, 1997 ff*

Aristotle, *various, ca. 360 BCE ff*

Augustine, *various, 386 ff*

Avicenna, *various, ca. 1020 ff*

Barrow, J.D., *The Book of Nothing, 2000*

Boethius, A.M.S., *The Consolation of Philosophy, 525*

The Bible, any version, first written version ca. 800 BCE ff

Chomsky, A.N., *various, 1957 ff*

Collins, F.S., *The Language of God, 2006*

Darwin, C.R., *various, 1839 ff*

Dawkins, R.S., *The God Delusion, 2006; et al. 1976 ff*

Einstein, A., *various, 1905 ff*

Forbes, W.E., *Cycles of Personal Belief, 1917*

Frost, R.L., *various, 1913 ff*

Gould, S.J., *Rocks of Ages, 1999*

Greenblatt, S.J., *The Rise and Fall of Adam and Eve, 2017*

Hawking, S.A., *A Brief History of Time, 1988; et al. 1970 ff*

Hegel, G.W.F., *Phenomenology of Spirit, 1807*

Heisenberg, W.K., *various, 1925 ff*

Huxley, A.L., *various, 1925 ff*

Jung, C.J., *various, ca. 1910 ff*

Lewis, C.S., *Mere Christianity, 1952; et al., ca. 1933 ff*

Nagel, T., *Mind and Cosmos, 2012*

Piaget, J.W.F., *various, 1923 ff*

Pinker, S.A., *The Better Angels of Our Nature, 2011; et al. 2018*

Plato, *Complete Works, 1997; et al. ca. 400 BCE ff*

Randall, L.J., *various, 2005 ff*

Sayers, D.L., *The Lost Tools of Learning, 1947*

Shakespeare, W., *various, ca. 1600*

Every book written has instruction for the attentive on the matters discussed.

Index

Index

Index

Index

About the Author

Spike Forbes lives in Sheridan, Wyoming, enjoying family and grandchildren. He graduated from Yale University with a degree in mathematics, followed by three years of teaching with the Peace Corps in Honduras and further study at Cornell, Colorado State and Sheridan Community College. Before retirement, his working life was in animal agriculture, applying statistical and mathematical theories to genetic and economic practices. His parents and lineage encouraged a thoughtful approach to all matters; the characters chosen for the book reflect that passion. He has enjoyed participation on library, school, church, county and national boards. Hobbies include continuing exploration, learning and friendships in philosophy, religion, science and agriculture.

Notes for the 2nd Edition

Three errors were uncovered in the first edition, one of substance and others of clarity. For clarity, the distinction may not have been as clear as it might have been between constructs, which have existence but can be perceived intact only by the single human in whose mind they reside as abstractions, versus objects, which have outside existence perceptible by any human (or other observer). Science may someday show that thoughts can be directly transmitted from one mind to another, for example by brain-waves. That finding might expand our means of communication, but limit them as it does so; the premises for this book would remain unchanged. Constructs and objects would continue as non-overlapping sets.

A great deal of wording has been changed for more clarity.

The substantial error was the failure to include a capability for action among the necessary attributes of an observer. That omission not only limits the nature of communication, but also limits the potential for relationship between two observers. It allowed only two processes for change, the slow one of natural evolution, and the (sometimes) exponential one of biology. Human action gives a third variable-speed alternative process.

The errors have no effect on the nature of any ematomic gaps.